The Artist's

Kent Nerburn is a sculptor and award-winning author of sixteen books. He has been writing about Native American history and culture for almost thirty years, and is the founder and director of 'Project Preserve', working on the Red Lake Ojibwe reservation helping students collect memories of tribal elders. He lives in Portland, Oregon.

kentnerburn.com

Also by Kent Nerburn

Calm Surrender
Chief Joseph and the Flight of the Nez Perce
Letters to My Son
Make Me an Instrument of Your Peace
Simple Truths
Small Graces
The Wolf at Twilight
Neither Wolf Nor Dog
Native Echoes
The Girl Who Sang to the Buffalo
Ordinary Sacred
Voices in the Stones

The Artist's Journey

On Making Art & Being an Artist

KENT NERBURN

CANONGATE

This trade paperback edition published in Great Britain,
the USA and Canada in 2020

First published in Great Britain, the USA and Canada in 2018
as *Dancing with the Gods* by Canongate Books Ltd,
14 High Street, Edinburgh EH1 1TE

Distributed in the USA by Publishers Group West and in
Canada by Publishers Group Canada

canongate.co.uk

2

British Library Cataloguing-in-Publication Data
A catalogue record for this book is available on
request from the British Library

ISBN: 978 1 78689 117 4

Typeset in Granjon by
Palimpsest Book Production Ltd, Falkirk, Stirlingshire

Printed and bound in Great Britain by Clays Ltd, Elcograf S.p.A.

MIX
Paper from
responsible sources
FSC
www.fsc.org   FSC® C018072

For Tom Kraabel, who believed in me, and
Wayne Rood, who taught me that art must care

Contents

THE HARD PLACES

THE HIDDEN SECRETS

THE UNSEEN JOYS

Art is a spiritual pursuit
It is wrestling with the angels
It is dancing with the gods

Introduction:

Dreams and Fears

Choosing the artist's life

'Inside you there's an artist
you don't know about.'
Rumi

RECENTLY I RECEIVED a note from a young woman named Jennifer who was questioning her decision to pursue a life in the arts. She had a dream, she felt a calling, but she was feeling alone and misunderstood.

'Is it worth it?' she asked. 'Is it possible? What advice can you give me?'

Her letter touched me. It mirrored the doubts and yearnings of my own youth. Though I couldn't tell her what to do, I wanted to respond.

This is what I wrote to her:

Dear Jennifer,
Thank you for your kind letter. You honour me by
thinking that I might have some advice to offer on

your questions about devoting your life to the arts. It takes great courage to reach out to a person you don't know because something in their work touches a chord in you and resonates with that private, unspoken place of your dreams. I know, because I did the same when I was younger. In my case, it was to Norman Mailer.

Why I chose Norman Mailer, I don't know. I certainly didn't find his emotional sensibilities attuned to mine. His work, though powerful, was not consonant with my own literary spirit. I think it was because there was a muscularity in his intellectual manner that I felt was lacking in my own life. I had just begun a graduate programme at Stanford University, and the combination of the intellectual demands of the academic life and the shock of a new living and learning environment – graduate school, at least at that time, was a far different animal than undergraduate school – made me feel ever further from the living streets and ordinary people where I felt most vibrant and alive. Mr Mailer's work probably gave me hope that there was a way to be intelligent without being an intellectual, and that a life on the streets did not negate a life of the mind.

Whatever it was, I wrote him, and though I do not have a copy of the letter, I can guess what I said. It was likely very much like your letter – confessional, almost pleading, a lifeline thrown to a person whose life and accomplishments seemed to resonate with what I wanted for myself and what so few others seemed to understand. I suppose I wanted a helping hand, or maybe an occupational road map, or maybe just the simple acknowledgement that my plight and dreams were real and worthy.

I do remember that I asked if I could come to New York and work with him – a request that makes me blush even now when I think of it. But Mr Mailer, gruff though he might have seemed in his public persona, wrote back with gentle compassion.

I have the note still today, written on a manual typewriter and signed with a fountain pen. I'll share it with you in its entirety because it speaks to the generosity of the man:

142 Columbia Heights
Brooklyn, N.Y.
19 March 1970

Dear Kent Nerburn:

Your letter is fine but I'm not going to respond to it.
I work alone and I think very little can be learned about writing being
in the neighborhood of another writer unless one uses a scribe and that
hardly seems a role for you. The heart of becoming a writer is to come
into focus on oneself. To know -- and usually it's best not to know
until after you've done it -- what has finally become important to
write about and what you can say that no one else particularly can
say. And that can take years and all sorts of occupations. But there's
no quick road to a focus like working. It's part of the hurdle, In
fact, it keeps most talented people from becoming real writers. Anyway,
you wrote your letter so long ago you're doubtless in a different mood.

Hope this finds you well. If you're in doubt, work. Write
more than you have been writing.

Sincerely,

Norman Mailer

I don't remember my immediate reaction. But I held on to that note like a drowning man holds on to a piece of passing wreckage. I was acknowledged; I was real; I was worthy of a response from a man whose life was inconceivably greater and more resolved than mine. Perhaps I was not going to drown.

I hope that by writing to you I can give you some of the same solace, because you are real, you are worthy, your dreams are worth pursuing. And you are not going to drown.

I know, because I have walked the same time-honoured path. All artists have. We have shared your doubts. We have wrestled the same demons and held the same dreams. And all of us would tell you the same thing: though it is not an easy journey, it is a journey worth taking.

You will live in a world of uncertainty, never knowing if your creations are good enough, always fearing financial cataclysm, unsure if your dreams are more than self-delusion, and vulnerable to feelings of persecution and self-doubt. You will see others with less talent accomplishing more and feel the sting of unwarranted criticism. You will feel angry, lonely, unappreciated, and misunderstood.

But you will also live in a world of joy, with its magical moments when the act of creation lifts you and propels you with a power that seems to come from beyond yourself. You will remain constantly vibrant and young at heart because your urge to create will keep your spirit alive and interested in the world around you long after others in other professions have become weary and soul-deadened in the monotonous sameness of their everyday lives. And you will own your own time, and know the miraculous experience of having intimate conversations with people long dead and far away through your personal dialogue with their art. You will know what it is to work with love.

Few people on the outside will understand the precarious nature of this life. They will see only the accolades and accomplishments, the apparent freedom and the finished products of your efforts.

They will not understand that the person who

creates something from the intimacy of their own imagination and places it before others as a gift of the creative spirit stands on the precipice of failure and rejection – or, worse yet, mediocrity – at every moment. That by creating a work of art – a performance, a painting, a piece of writing or anything else – you have, metaphorically speaking, brought a child into the world, and the rejection of a child of your creation hurts you with the pain of a parent watching their child be ignored, demeaned, and seen as unworthy.

These are things that you will come to know if you devote yourself to a life in the arts. It is not a life for everyone. But if you have the courage to choose it, you will have embarked upon one of life's great adventures. You will have joined the tribe of the dreamers, the keepers of the stories, the shapers of visions and caretakers of the imagination. You will have chosen to set your sights on the stars.

I hope you will choose to become one of us. We come from many different backgrounds, with many *different talents and many different dreams. But there is one truth we all share. If we had it to do again, we would choose the very same path.*

This is a life truly worth living.

All my best,

Kent

When I had finished my response, I sat back and read what I had written. It seemed good, and it felt good. With luck, my letter would touch Jennifer as Norman Mailer's letter had touched me and would help her chart a course in life that was worthy of her dreams.

I sealed it up and sent it off.

But I continued to be haunted by the earnest hunger and yearning of her words. That she had reached out to me, sharing her deepest fears and dreams, was both humbling and daunting.

I kept thinking back to a time several years before when I had been asked to participate in a sweat lodge with some Lakota friends deep in the hills of the Pine Ridge Indian reservation in western South Dakota. They were honouring me for my thirty years of working as an ally of the Native people. By sheer coincidence, the sweat took place on the day of my sixtieth birthday. It gave even greater meaning to an already profound experience.

A sweat lodge is not something to be taken lightly. It is a ceremony of deep significance – a religious practice, actually – meant to cleanse and clarify those who attend. It should be undertaken only with an open heart.

In the course of the ceremony in the almost unbearable heat of the pitch-dark lodge, everyone is asked to speak what is in their heart. When my turn came, I said, almost without thinking, 'I want to learn how to be an elder.' I meant it in the most profound sense of the term.

Over the years, I had become close to the Native people and immersed in their way of understanding. For them, life is not a straight line from birth to death, with the time of central importance being the years in the middle, but a circle, like the seasons, where each age has its gifts and responsibilities. The elders, as the only ones who have experienced all the seasons of life, have the responsibility of sharing the wisdom they have gained on their life's journey.

Jennifer's letter had brought that experience back to me. As I reflected on her letter and the others like it I had received over the years, I realised that the time had come for me to take on the responsibility I had prayed about in that sweat lodge. It was time for me to speak, as an elder and a teacher, about what it means to live a life in the arts.

I had spent thirty years living the life of the writer, and twenty before that as a practising sculptor. I knew the heart of the artistic life – its dreams and fears, its unspoken challenges, and its unexpected rewards. It was time to share my thoughts about what it meant to live the life of the artist, so that not only Jennifer but all the Jennifers of the world – and all those who had once been like Jennifer but had been forced to put their artistic dreams on hold, or those who had come late to the artistic journey – could learn from my experience and have a glimpse into the magic that a life in the arts offers.

And so this book was born.

In it I try to share, with as much honesty as I can, some of what I have learned on my artistic journey. I offer it to all of you who have fallen under the spell of the arts and dream of giving voice to the creative spirit that lives inside of you. But most of all I offer it as a gift to you who are just beginning on your artistic journey and feel the arts pulling on you, like the moon pulls on the tides, and want to know something of what your journey will be like.

To all of you, and any others who wish to have a glimpse into this life that so many admire and so few understand, I offer these words with an open heart.

May they give you insight, inspiration, and courage.

I hope you find them worthy of your time.

THE JOURNEY
BEGINS

1

Courting the Muse

Finding the place where time stands still

*'To this day I do not know whether the power
which has inspired my works is something related
to religion, or is indeed religion itself'*
Kathe Kollwitz

*'. . . when I am alone with my notes, my heart
pounds and the tears stream from my eyes, and my
emotion and my joys are too much to bear.'*
Giuseppe Verdi

I REMEMBER THE moment. It was ten o'clock on a warm August night in a small German town. I was alone in the workshop of an antique restorer who had generously allowed me to help in his shop so I could learn German for my American graduate school. Everyone else had gone home for the evening.

I was standing before an old, battered workbench. A string of electric lights flickered on a single cord above my head. With the streets outside dark and quiet, I was as alone as a man in a foreign country, with no friends or family or familiar language, can be.

On the bench in front of me lay a piece of maple – a slab about three feet long, two feet wide, and maybe six inches thick. It had been given to me by the workshop owner when I had asked, tentatively, if I could perhaps use some of his chisels to try my hand at woodcarving.

I had taken to visiting the local churches and folk museums and had found myself transfixed by the old crucifixes carved by devout peasants and farmers, probably to while away the dark German nights of the Late Middle Ages. The carvings had been so filled with heart, so honest in their spiritual yearning. I, who was in graduate school for the study of religion, and deeply unfilled by the academic dissection of human faith, had found in them a spiritual presence that I experienced nowhere else. Nothing in my experience had prepared me for the effect these works had on my heart and imagination.

I did not know how to carve. I did not even know how to hold the chisels. But somewhere inside of me I had a vision born of those many visits to the museums and churches, and of the deep spiritual hunger and loneliness that was surrounding my life so far from home.

With a first stroke, I cut into the piece of maple.

The mallet in my hand made a hollow sound as it hit the butt of the chisel. The wood moved and a shaving curled up. I hit the chisel again, moving yet another chip of wood. Then another. I dug into that wood with no understanding of what I was doing. I only knew that something was alive and waiting to be released from inside the block of wood on the bench before me.

I hit the mallet again and again, seeking something I could apprehend but could not see. The wood moved, the block changed; inchoate forms took shape in my mind's eye.

When at last I was too tired to continue, I looked up. The clock on the wall said 5 a.m. I had been standing over that bench for seven hours and I had experienced no passage of time.

At that moment I understood, for the first time in my life, something about the magic of art. Each hour spent in my books in graduate school was difficult. Some were fascinating, filling me with new thoughts and ideas. But none had ever annihilated my sense of time.

This experience bordered on the mystical. I did not want to stop; I did not want to sleep. Only my weariness caused me to put down the chisels and make my way back to my garret room. I could hardly wait to return and begin again.

Since that time, as both a sculptor and a writer, this ecstatic annihilation has called to me, beckoning me with the promise of being taken out of myself and transported to a place where I am nothing more than a vehicle for a vision.

All artists know this experience. This, more than almost anything else, is why we do what we do. It is an occasion of grace, and, once experienced, it holds with a power that will not let go.

This is also the reason why artists often speak of their work in religious terms. To be lifted out of yourself – to be taken up and used for what feels like a higher purpose – is to feel, if only for a moment, that you are participating in the creative power of the universe. You are held in the hand of something greater than yourself.

All of us want this experience. It is what lifts our

work from craft to art, moves it into the realm of the spiritual and silences the critic who whispers constantly from our shoulder. It is the embrace of the incandescent present.

Artists have many ways of courting this embrace. Some have a ritual of preparation – from the simple way they lay out the work before them to a period of deep prayer or meditation. Some have physical spaces they have set aside where only their creative work can take place. Some work in silence; some surround themselves with music.

Japanese sword makers, seeking not ecstasy but clarity in their tradition of spiritual discernment, have a time-honoured and elaborate ritual of preparation and entry that becomes a portal to creative forces beyond themselves.

All of these have the same purpose: to put you inside the act of creation, so you are not making art, but art is being revealed through you.

If you would make a life in the arts, you must find a way to enter into this state. Chances are you have already experienced it, ever so slightly, while immersed in the practice of your art. Very likely it is what has driven you to dream of the artistic life.

But understand – just as there are days when you live in the presence of the creative spirit, there will be days when all your efforts turn to dust. Your work will seem false, your inspiration clouded. Instead of walking into a garden of imaginative possibilities, you will find yourself plodding through dry places where nothing seems able to grow.

Do not let the dry stretches and arid days deter you. They will come and go at their whim, and there is little you can do to change their course except to push with discipline during those times when you cannot proceed with grace, and to prepare, through ritual and spiritual focus, for the moment when once again you can be taken up into the joyful immediacy of creation.

What you cannot do is let yourself fall under the sway of the romantic notion that you should work only when filled with inspiration. Inspiration is a cruel mistress and a wily deceiver, and waiting for it will turn you into a lazy artist. Sometimes you must rely only on your own will to drive you forward.

Whether those times of working from sheer force of will produce good art or only prepare the ground for more inspired creation in the future is not for you to say. Yours is only to work, by such lights as you have, seeking the moment when once again you are not making art but art is speaking through you.

Remember this: if, in the act of creation, you find yourself, just for a moment, losing all sense of time and being lifted up into a great, all-embracing 'Yes!' where there is neither past nor future but only the magical and incandescent present, you have found the place where creation takes wing.

Honour this, seek this, court this. Do whatever you need to do to find that place where you inhabit your art and your art inhabits you. Then claim it and name it and find a way to call it forth – whether by establishing a space dedicated only to your work, or establishing a ritual of preparation and entry, or any other act that takes you away from the concerns of daily life and opens the door to the place where the muse sits on your shoulder.

When you find it, cherish it. In its own distant fashion, it is perhaps the closest we can come to a touch with the divine.

2

Finding a Vision, Finding a Voice

The search for authentic personal expression

'There is a vitality, a life force, an energy, a quickening that is translated through you into action, and because there is only one of you in all time, this expression is unique. And if you block it, it will never exist through any other medium and will be lost'

Martha Graham

I ONCE HAD a dear friend, a painter, who had magic in his hands. I looked with envy upon the ease and grace with which he could craft an image on canvas. I dreamed of someday having the same ease and grace in my own work.

One night, after a long bout of drinking, he broke down and began to unburden himself to me. Painting, he said, came easily to him. His capacity to shape human forms was like a God-given gift. Seemingly without effort he produced images that could have stood next to the works of Dante Gabriel Rossetti and the pre-Raphaelites. But he was miserably unhappy.

'How can you be unhappy?' I asked. 'You have such a talent.'

'Oh, Kent,' he said. 'You don't understand. If only I had something to say, I could say it so well.'

Those words have haunted me ever since.

It was as if he had some artistic mark of Cain upon his forehead, some perverse curse dreamed up by a vengeful god. He dreamed of being a great painter, but he felt he was nothing more than a masterful technician, and for him that was not enough.

Most of us don't carry the burden of having too much talent for our artistic dreams. Usually we are driven to create by some great inner urge, hungry for external expression. Our struggle is not finding something to say, but finding the skill with which to say it.

For years, I felt sadness for my friend's apparent lack of an artistic inner life. But as I've got older, I've come to realise that he did not lack an inner life, he merely had become tyrannised by what he thought his art ought to be. He did not see the genius in his hands as art enough and did not accept his artistic creations as reflective of a worthy artistic vision.

This happens to many of us. We study the work of those who have inspired us and try to imitate it.

We project a fantasy of what great art is, or how an artist should act, and try to replicate it. In the end, we become copyists, no matter how skilled, because our work does not have an authentic heart; it references the artistry of others. No matter how much those works we reference speak to our own creative vision, we do not own them. They did not come forth from our own creative experience. We have become creative plagiarists.

There is no shame in drawing on the works of others as we develop our own voice and vision. It is, in fact, a great compliment to those who have inspired us. The danger we face is that those works touched us in a fundamental way, but we do not have either the aesthetic range or depth of human understanding to transcend them, or that they are simply an ill-fitting suit of artistic clothes for the artistic talent or temperament that we possess. We do not become the students who surpass the master, just the students who imitate the master. At some point, we need to step forth from their shadow and find our own voice.

I have another friend, also a visual artist, who creates

beautiful pencil drawings that evoke images of cities and landscapes as seen from far above the earth. They are both lyrical and meditative, at once abstract and realistic. They engage the mind and enchant the eye.

One day I asked him how he had developed such an amazing artistic vision.

'I don't really have any artistic vision,' he said. 'I just draw the reflections I see in the subway windows when I'm riding.'

I appreciated his humility but could not believe there was not more to his work than that. I told him how his drawings awakened images in me of a land-scape seen from high above the earth.

'Maybe,' he shrugged, 'but that's not what I make. I just draw the reflections I see in the subway windows.'

For him, grand meaning or significant metaphor was not a necessary purpose of his art. His was the art of close inspection, the art of simple observation. It was not the art of great ideas. He was a translator. He took the world as he saw it and gave it back to us. And that, for him, was enough.

How I wish my first friend had been so at peace

with his creative talents. But he was not at peace with his art because he was not at peace with himself as an artist. Beneath that magical talent was a man in search of his place in the world.

There is no law that says art must express grand human themes or point beyond itself to larger meanings. For many artists the simple gestures of life, closely observed, are sufficient. I have heard it said that there are actors whose entire method of character development is to figure out how their character talks and moves, and then try to inhabit those mannerisms. When they get them right, they are done. They just walk the walk, talk the talk, say the lines. They have no feeling for the inner life of their characters and no wish to have any. The objective reality, and what it expresses, is enough.

For others, it is only by entering into the mind and soul of the character and having that knowledge illuminate each gesture and action that they can create authentic expression.

I am sure the same is true also for dancers. I know it is true for singers.

It is important to remind ourselves that what is central in any art form is not the scale or intent of our vision but the authenticity of that vision.

I remember a time twenty years ago when I was teaching a class on creativity in the arts and I asked a young woman to find an experience of grief or love in her life, then to find a painting or piece of music that gave voice to that emotion.

She was a weaver and I wanted her to experience an expressive kinship with the work of other artists in other fields. But she was having none of it.

'I don't care about that,' she said. 'My art isn't about deep feelings, it's about making things people like.'

For her, creating beauty through sensitive use of colour and texture and form and line was sufficient. She had no need – indeed, no desire – to place deep meaning in her work. Deep meaning, if there was to be any, was to be found in the way her work enhanced the lives of others by making them happy and enriching their visual environment. Her work had no more inherent significance than an inviting hearth fire, and she was proud to claim that humble simplicity.

It took me a long time to understand that gentle, almost domestic approach to the arts. As a creator myself, I, like so many, laboured under the belief that my art should have profound significance. It was not enough to be good; I had to be great. But through people like my student I eventually came to realise that though greatness may be a worthy dream, it is not a valid measure. Greatness is an idea, a status conferred by others. It is not something you can seek. If you fit inside the shape of your art and work with a committed heart, that is enough.

I wish my friend with the magic in his hands had known this. But he was still in thrall to the vision of others. He had not taken his magnificent talent and fit it into an aesthetic vessel that he could claim as his own.

Not all art has to address eternal questions. Art, any art, can live by touching some common human sentiment in us as surely as it can live by touching some deep emotional taproot. To inspire, to console, to reveal, to calm, or simply to entertain – these, and so many others, are worthy artistic purposes. The genius of art is that it can meet us where we live, and the joy of creation is that we can choose the place where we want our art to touch those who experience it.

My friend was a gentle soul with a gentle outlook on life. He should have been satisfied to express that gentleness through his amazing talent. It was not that he had nothing to say, he just hadn't realised that what he had to say was enough.

What he had not grasped is that art is ultimately about giving authentic expression to what lives in your heart. People sense authenticity, even if they can't quantify it or articulate how they recognise its presence. But they know it, and they relate to it, because authenticity has a spiritual resonance that we all understand.

If you can find what it is that you can say through your art that no one else can say in quite the same way, you are getting close to finding your authentic artistic voice.

Perhaps you feel the need to address the whole of the human condition. Perhaps you only want to decorate space or add warmth to the life of a family or put a smile on people's faces. Perhaps you wish to do nothing more than transcribe what you see in a subway window. What matters is the quality of heart in your work, and the authenticity of the voice in which you speak.

If you are able to find that authentic voice and you have the courage to believe in it, you will never have to lament that you have nothing to say. Even if your voice is small and your intentions humble, what you say will be heard.

Too many artists, in trying to mimic another's voice, find in the end that they have merely rendered themselves mute.

3

Inspiration and Training

The essential responsibility
of learning your craft

*'There are two men inside the artist, the poet
and the craftsman. One is born a poet.
One becomes a craftsman.'*
Emile Zola

*'Be a good craftsman; it won't stop
you from being a genius.'*
Pierre-Auguste Renoir

IF SOMEONE TELLS you there is but one way to create or one way to find your artistic voice, be wary. They may have a technique or method that works for them, and you should always listen to what they have to say – after all, the essence of being an artist is to be open to the full richness of the world around us. But if they say, 'This is the way it must be done,' listen with caution. Take their words as a reflection of their confidence in their own method of creation but don't allow them to distort your own vision or control your own search for the wellspring of your art.

This is not to say that you should ignore the techniques and methods of others. Much good can be gained by putting yourself in the hands of a teacher who has a definite and specific way of creating. Though you may chafe at his or her methods, you will benefit greatly from giving yourself to them. You will learn the discipline of working against your own inclinations and open yourself to a new way of shaping the external world into a work of art.

After all, any teacher who has lived a long life in the arts has hard-won knowledge, and the lessons he or she has to teach will imprint your work for the better, even if you choose to take a different direction on your own artistic journey. The talent you need is to know what lessons to take and which to leave behind as you move forward on your own artistic path.

Many years ago I trained under a woodcarver who specialised in iconostases, or altar screens, for Orthodox churches. The iconostases he created were often twelve feet high and twenty feet long, and consisted entirely of intertwined stems and leaves done in a traditional Byzantine style. He had learned this craft as a child in his native Greece and had spent forty years perfecting his methods and techniques. His creations were impeccable.

Though he claimed he could do other kinds of works, he could not, because he was singularly lacking in artistic imagination. He was a craftsman – a brilliant craftsman – who could carve a perfectly smooth surface and cut a perfectly clean line in the middle of a stylised leaf such that the line, made without measurement, was exactly equidistant from either side of the leaf's edge.

This may not sound like much, and in the scheme of what I dreamed of doing as a sculptor it was not. But in training with him I was forced to accept the mind-numbing discipline of carving leaf after leaf with unerring exactitude, though my heart dreamed of creating life-size human forms in the tradition of Donatello and Michelangelo, and I chafed under the limitations of his exacting demands. But unbeknownst to me I was gaining a rigour and discipline that, once learned, would undergird everything I would do in the future as a sculptor.

Because of this man and his training I could give exactly the right line and shape to an eyelid to create a feeling of sadness and moral complexity in the rendering of a human face. He had taught me nothing about embodying human emotions and expressions in wood, but his training had allowed me to have the technical control necessary to make the precise millimetre of cut that would make the difference between bringing something to life and merely making it accurate.

Without that man's harsh training – and it was harsh, to the point of him threatening to break my fingers if I did not do things the way he wanted – I would never have been able to bring the visions to life that I held inside me once I was set free to create on my own. What he was doing was putting skills in my hands that would allow me to give voice to the art in my heart.

As young artists we are too quick to want to run to the well of pure creative expression. We do not want to subject ourselves to training that seems to run contrary to the creative fire that burns inside us. Whether it be technical discipline and exacting craftsmanship, such as I was subjected to by my carving teacher, or techniques demanded by a voice coach or dancing instructor or writing mentor who insists that we follow a certain course of study, the training we are getting is playing a crucial role in helping us develop our own unique artistic voice. It is giving us a foundation on which to build, and helping us develop as artists by making us realise what we are not.

Leonardo da Vinci once said it is a poor teacher whose students do not surpass the master. Your goal as a creator is to make your mentors into good teachers by surpassing them on your artistic journey. Just remember to thank them, with your words, with your art, with your acknowledgements. They let you stand on their shoulders, as they stood on the shoulders of those before them. Whether they gently lifted you down and sent you on your way, or you leapt before they thought you were ready, they gave you the gift of their experience.

It is up to you to use it, to honour it, and, ultimately, to pass it on.

4

Dancing over the Abyss

The courage to fail

'Creativity takes courage'
Henri Matisse

THERE IS ART and there is artistry, and they are not the same.

Artistry is raising an act to a level of proficiency and clarity that allows it to shine with a brilliance that others performing the same act seldom achieve. It is seeing through to the heart of an activity and performing it with mindfulness and excellence. The artistry of the surgeon, the artistry of the homemaker, the artistry of the mechanic and the machinist are all expressions of this urge toward excellence.

Art is something different. It is creating something unique, never before seen or heard; a child, freshly born, adding a new voice to the chorus of creation. It is fragile and moves on unsteady legs, uncertain of its place, or even if it has a place at all. It differs from artistry in that artistry is an elevation, a consecration of the ordinary. It can lose its balance, fall back and take its place among the everyday, and both the creator and the world may be lesser for its falling, but there is no loss, no death, only the dimming of the light of excellence.

But a work of art, if it fails, is a death. It is a failure of the pieces to coalesce in that incandescent alchemy that turns a stone to gold. You are left holding failure in your hands. It is a lonely and painful experience.

The willingness to take this risk is the great unseen courage of the artist. When people on the outside see an artist's nervousness, or curtness, or quirky behaviour, they often write it off as neurosis or self-absorption. What they are really seeing is the external expression of the artist's struggle to walk that knife-edge of risk to arrive at that perfect creative pitch that will give their creation life. They don't understand that they are seeing a struggle between artistic life and death.

Stories abound of performers who would vomit

before going onstage, or, finding something amiss in their performance, quit in mid-sentence or mid-note and walk off, not to return to performing for years or perhaps for the remainder of their lives. This sort of anxiety is but the overflow of the creative tension that attends an attempt to create something where failure is a kind of death.

Every artist knows this feeling in some degree. Whether a painter in the studio or a dancer preparing to go onstage, you whipsaw between boundless hopes and utter dejection because you have known the magic of the inspiration that gave birth to your work and you know the death that will take place if you fail to give it adequate voice.

When a performer walks off stage in mid-performance, a painter slashes a canvas, or an author tears up a manuscript, it is just the action of a person who is facing the sudden awareness that their work has no life and is spiralling into despondency because something that had so much promise and in which they had so much faith suddenly lies dead in their hands.

There is nothing you can do to chase this terror

away, but there is much you can do to reduce it to a fine-tuned vigilance and a harp-string readiness. It has to do with self-mastery and faith.

You would not be where you are and your creation would not have reached the point where it had potential for life had there not been a core of artistry that gave it birth. Your fear is that the artistry that informed it is not enough; that there is only the abyss of artistic death on the other side of failure.

But you must keep in mind that where there is artistry, failure will never be absolute. Our artistry is alive, even if in imperfect form, every time we create. We may despair at the imperfection of our creation, or sink into a depression at its failure to adequately reflect our vision, but these are responses only to perceived mediocrity, not to total failure.

Your work, even at its weakest, contains within it the kernel of life. When you allow your fear or your insecurity or your unrealistic belief in perfection to control you, you are betraying that possibility of life. You are saying that you do not have faith in the artistic child born of the union between your imagination and your talent. You are measuring your art by your own standards of excellence rather than trusting your art and letting it make its way into the hearts of others by its own devices.

I once had a professor who took me aside after listening to me lament about the deficiencies in my work. 'It's time for you to put those thoughts away,' he said. 'Treat your art like a friend. Focus on its strengths, not its weaknesses.' This is worthy counsel, and, hard though it is to do, I try to live by it every time I set my hand to some new act of creation.

I cannot tell you that the fear ever goes away, or that the precipice over which you stand ever disappears. And I don't pretend that you can ignore that precipice any more than you could ignore a canyon beneath you as you try to make your way across a narrow bridge spanning its chasm.

But you need to trust that your art, once created, has a value apart from you, just as a child, come into the world, has a value separate from the parents who gave it life. When you give in to self-loathing, insecurity, or stage fright, you are looking at your work from the outside, and the outside is a shapeless darkness that contains all your self-doubt and fears.

The ideal is a concept. Perfection is for angels. Failure is absolute only if you deny the fundamental artistry that lies at the heart of your art. People will often comment on mistakes and missteps because they are easier to see and articulate than abstractions like quality and excellence. But, at heart, most people sense your courage and want you to succeed. Only the small-minded among them will focus on your weaknesses to the exclusion of the overall sense of respect they feel in the presence of something they, themselves, would not dare attempt.

When the demons of fear and insecurity beset you, and they will, do not focus on the fumblings and missteps of your art but on the spirit that gave it birth. The artistry at the heart of your creation will always raise your work above the ordinary affairs of the day. And it is not for you to say whether or not your work has life: that is between your work – the child of your creation now living a life of its own – and those who encounter it.

Remember, you believed in the spirit of your work when you first brought it to life. There is no reason to doubt it now. Even if you did not give it a form as fully realised as you had hoped, or stumbled in its voicing, you must trust that some of that spirit is still there to be found.

It is, by and large, a trust that will prove to be well placed.

5

The Unwavering Beacon

The inviolable imperative of excellence

'In art, the best is good enough.'
Johann Wolfgang von Goethe

'An artist cannot do anything slovenly.'
Jane Austen

OUR FEELINGS ABOUT any work we create wax and wane. Some days we are filled with enthusiasm for it; other days it seems dull and lifeless. Some nights I will go to bed excited about what I left unfinished only to wake in the morning and find it insipid and incoherent. In the same fashion, I will discard a work as turgid or fragmentary, only to go back to it several months later and find a beauty in it that leaves me wondering what it was that had caused me to discard it in the first place.

We are often the worst judges of our own work. Either we see its deficiencies in high relief or we overestimate its capacity to express what we set out to reveal. We are too close to it and too invested in it to see its strengths and weaknesses.

How are we to know if what we have done is good? The hard truth is that we can't. If you are the type of artist who values audience response or external success, perhaps those are viable measures. But if you are like most of us, you are harder on yourself than anyone else is. And you have not arrived at where you are by minimising your weaknesses. So you see your work poorly, if at all.

What I would like to suggest is that if there is no reliable measure of quality, there is one reliable internal measure that you can still use as a guide. It is excellence.

Excellence is a habit — it is a mode of creating. It is fluid and it is malleable in its expression, but it is consistent in its intention. If you establish the habit of excellence in your work, it will always be there, no matter how distant you feel from that work or how flawed it felt in the act of creation.

Excellence cannot be quantified and it is different for each person. It is where your character shines through your creation. It is your commitment, frozen in time and space. It is your spiritual signature on your work.

A true artist should never dismiss the imperative of excellence. An acquaintance of mine – one who, blessedly, was not in an artistic field – used to brag that in any task his intention was 'to do just enough not to embarrass himself'. Such a person should never be allowed to get near the sacred responsibility of art. The only honourable position of any artist is to be as present as possible to every act of creation and to treat each work as if it is the last they will ever create.

I remember a substantial argument I once had with the director of an internationally recognised choral ensemble that was giving a performance in the small town where I was living. I accused him of pandering to our rural audience by offering us the vacuous musical fare of show tunes and ragtime rather than the profoundly beautiful works of medieval and Renaissance polyphony for which his group was so justly renowned.

'You don't take us seriously,' I said. 'You presume our rural location reflects a lack of sophistication, when we are the ones who are most starved for the music you create. We're just a throwaway performance for you.'

He took great offence at my assumption. 'Nothing is a throwaway performance for us,' he said. 'We take this as seriously as a performance in Lincoln Center.'

And his indignation was legitimate. Even if the programming lacked sophistication and the stakes were small, he would never allow his ensemble to pursue anything less than absolute excellence in any performance, no matter what the venue. He had the heart and commitment of a true artist.

As you progress through your artistic life, you will discover that the works you create leave tracks. Though you do not work for a legacy, you create one. Your work becomes a history of your time on earth. It is like a string of pearls, formed of the works you have created or the performances you have given; a family of your artistic children. Not all came forth equal in form and grace. Some came into being more easily; some took on a life of their own more swiftly and with more certainty. But in the end they are your legacy and your history, and your reason for having been here.

It is easy to become focused on the more external aspects of our artistic efforts – Will people like my work? Will it sell? Will it advance my career? – or to get caught up in fruitless attempts to decide if our work has any inherent merit. But if you keep your eye always on the challenge of making every work excellent within the constraints that are placed on you, whether by deadlines, the shape of the project or your own capacity to achieve the ends you envision, you are setting an internal standard that is impervious to outside influences.

When you reach the point in life's journey where you turn and look back on what you have done, what will matter is the way your spirit shone through the works you created. You may blush at the naivety of some of them and you may be astonished at the sophistication of others. You may say, 'I wish I could do that one over,' or you may say, 'How did I do that? I could never do that again.' But what is important is that you are able to say that each one reflected the greatest excellence of which you were capable at the time.

Time changes our perspective. We find our aesthetics, our interests, and our skills have moved far from where we began. But excellence, since it is the highest expression of our creative capability, becomes our unique artistic signature. It shines through all our artistic endeavours and forms a luminous thread that unites them.

At the end of your artistic life, you want to be able to say, in the words of the Book of Genesis, that you looked back upon the works of your creation and saw that they were good. If you were present to each, and invested each with the fullness of your creative spirit, you will be able to claim this legacy. You will be able to face the world and say, 'I gave you and my art the best I had.'

As an artist, you can know no greater peace, and it is a peace that is entirely in your hands to create.

THE HARD
PLACES

6

The Peril of Easy Blessing

The need for long patience
and the pitfalls of early success

'Adopt the pace of nature:
her secret is patience.'
Ralph Waldo Emerson

'It takes a long time to bring excellence
to maturity.'
Publilius Syrus

THERE IS A great difference between success and accomplishment. Success is an external measure of fame or financial reward. It is a ratification by the outside world that what you have done and, by extension, who you are, has mattered. Accomplishment is the body of work, the achievement of the life, the fruit of long patience and the steadfast fulfilment of the artistic journey. And it may or may not correspond in any fashion with success.

This is bitter gruel for many artists to swallow, for without the financial benefits and the reflected praise of external success our labours too often seem hopeless, worthless and without purpose. To labour in obscurity, finding satisfaction only from the mere act of creation, seems like a life only half lived.

Still, we should not be too hungry for success. Early success often contains a false promise. It is full of excitement and immediate passion. But, almost unnoticed, it begins to turn your focus to what works rather than to the authenticity of your art. Those who have discovered you want you to replicate what you have already done. Your art begins to harden, to take form too soon. It is an aesthetic binding of the feet, impelling something that still should be growing toward a final form when it should be expanding and flowering.

This is one of the great and unappreciated gifts of labouring in anonymity and obscurity: your work is allowed to mature. You are free to experiment, to try different voices, to put on different artistic identities. It frees you from the pressure of outside scrutiny and allows you to make mistakes without looking upon them as failures.

Yet working without success requires great strength of character. You must have faith that there is the spark of authentic talent within you. You must be able to persevere with only the love of your art as a driving force. These are strengths that many people, even people of great talent, simply don't have.

You need to remind yourself that patience is one of life's greatest virtues and one of nature's most fundamental truths. Nothing comes to full blossom before its time. Trying to force your art, or having it forced by the relentless demands of success, can often cause the blossoming to be false and fragile and less than it ultimately could be. As the artist Jean Arp said, we must let our art ripen inside us, like fruit on a vine or a child in its mother's womb.

Wabasha, the great Native American leader of the Dakotah people, advised his young people to 'guard your tongue in youth and in age you may mature a thought that will be of service to your people'.

We, as artists, should hold this counsel close to our hearts.

Listen to your inner urgings toward quality more than to the louder voices demanding success. The hunger for success is impatient, anxious, and clamorous. The urge toward meaningful accomplishment is steady, circumspect, and indifferent to recognition. Success dies with us; accomplishment lives on.

If you would create work that will live beyond you, learn the lessons of nature and cultivate the virtue of long patience. Better to labour quietly in the darkness than to be too soon exposed to the light.

7

Dark Nights and Waterless Places

When inspiration fails and doubt sets in

'I don't believe anyone ever suspects how completely unsure I am of my work and myself and what tortures of self-doubting the doubt of others has always given me.'
Tennessee Williams

'Our doubts are traitors,
And make us lose the good we oft might win
By fearing to attempt.'
William Shakespeare

THERE COMES A time in all of our artistic lives when we are overcome by weariness. We feel that we have worked too much and accomplished too little. We feel persecuted and misunderstood. We see others with less talent achieving more success and recognition, and we hurt for the sacrifices made by others who have stood by us as we pursued our dreams.

We are, quite simply, tired.

For the first time in our lives we begin to question whether it is worth the price. For the first time, we begin to wonder if we should quit.

This is no idle question, and it is not to be dismissed out of hand.

But before you make any decision I want you to

consider what I have to say. It may not be what you expect to hear.

There is nothing inherently noble about sacrificing the good of those around you and the people you love in pursuit of a dream. If the day comes when the dream of being an artist seems once and for all out of reach, or the harm to yourself and others too great, or the lure reveals itself to be a self-absorbed obsession, you need make no apology for choosing to take another path.

We are all fascinated, to some extent, with the artistic life. The artist is a beacon, a vision that rises above the workaday world and aims the heart toward the stars. Who would not dream of such a life?

But do not delude yourself. The teacher and the nurse do more immediate good in this world than the artist, any artist. They hold the hands of the lonely and mend the spirits of the broken. They shape the hearts and minds of the children. By the very tasks they perform each day they are serving as their brothers' and sisters' keepers. And the same can be said for many who labour in other pursuits.

You do a disservice to yourself and those around you if you think that the life of the creative artist is the only worthy life to live. That is a romantic concept that disrespects the greatness of a life of service or honest labour. But, more than that, it denies the fundamental truth that there is the potential for artistic expression in every field and every path of life.

We do not confer the mantle of artist on the counsellor or the surgeon or the homemaker or the carpenter because we do not see what they do as fitting into our definition of art. We grant them competence and excellence – worthy attributions, to be sure – but we do not accord their accomplishments the same status we give to a novelist or a dancer or a musician.

But the teacher who knows the exact moment to challenge or praise a child, the mother who knows when to support and when to discipline, the father who knows when to let go and let a child fly free, are making choices every bit as artistic as the painter choosing a palette or the actor choosing a gesture. But we fail to see them as artists because we look upon art as something external, brought forth from the imagination, and placed in the world. We do not see it as a perfecting of the ordinary.

This is understandable. There is a magic in the act of creating something where before there was nothing. It echoes, in a small and distant way, the great creative and generative force that animates the universe. When you touch that force by creating something new from nothing, you feel, if only for a moment, the presence of that force running through you, and you know in your heart that you have brushed against something fundamental in life.

But creativity has another dimension. It is the dimension of raising the ordinary to the level of pure artistry. The cultures of the East have understood this for centuries, and have a broader, more pervasive view of the artistic life. If you embrace, as they do, the understanding of art as the elevation of the ordinary to the level of the singular and the unique, all pursuits in life have the potential for artistry within them.

Perhaps you have neither the gift nor temperament to create art *ex nihilo* from the imagination. Perhaps you have the gift of making art by raising the ordinary to a level of clarity and mindful beauty. This type of art touches the earth in a more fundamental way, and offers a path to make any life lived with mindfulness and excellence into a life of art.

When times of weariness and aridity come to you as an artist, look closely into your heart to see if perhaps this is just the natural ebb and flow of creative energy, for times of weariness come to us all. But do not dismiss the possibility that this is your heart telling you that your talents and temperament might be better served by a life more closely tied to the world as it already exists than to a life wrestling with the unseen angels of creative possibility.

Artistic expression takes many forms and finds voice in every dimension of life. If you need to walk away from a life in the arts, do not be afraid to do so. There are many ways to live our lives and each has within it a magic and importance that no other can have. And each has within it the potential for artistry. Perhaps you may even find that your art will blossom more fully when carried on in the broader context of a life of service or labour quite unrelated to the arts.

What you have done and what you have experienced in the practice of your art will never leave you. It taught you what it means to be alive with an inner passion and how to live your life with mindful attention. And everything in life has its own time and its own season.

If you are meant to come back to your art, you will do so.

And you will not have to find your art, your art will find you.

8

The Slamming Door

The pain and challenge of rejection

*'Care about what other people think
and you will always be their prisoner'*
Lao Tzu

*'Art . . . is an area where it is impossible to walk
without stumbling. There are in store for you many
unsuccessful days and whole unsuccessful seasons:
there will be great misunderstandings and deep
disappointments . . . you must be prepared for all
this, expect it and nevertheless, stubbornly,
fanatically follow your own way.'*
Anton Chekhov

You will not have to journey far along the path of the artistic life before you receive a note or a phone call about a manuscript you submitted, an audition you made, or a competition you entered. It will begin something like this: 'Thank you for sharing your work with us. Unfortunately . . .'

This rejection will hit you like a blow because your expectation was filled with hope, and hope is life. All the emotions of grief will well up in you: anger, disbelief, and a lonely, private sadness.

Perhaps you will be resilient and take the blow with grace.

Perhaps you will be fragile and unsure and will find in the rejection a confirmation of your greatest fears — that you are mediocre and without talent. Perhaps you will believe, if only for a moment, that the struggle is not worth pursuing and you will want to quit.

Do not feel alone. All of us have been there.

One of the hard truths of a life in the arts is that each of us, in some secret corner of our heart, harbours the silent belief that we contain greatness within us. At the same time we live with the private fear that when all is stripped away we are mediocrities with little to say and no ability to say it.

When we experience rejection, our fears of mediocrity and charlatanism come rushing to the fore, leaving us ashamed and humiliated. We are overwhelmed with the self-doubt that has been lurking around the corners of our creative efforts, and we feel naked, unworthy, and unmasked.

Though these feelings lessen with age and experience, they never go away completely. But if we take a step back and allow the rejection to forge and temper us rather than destroy us, it can be a learning experience.

Remember that any creative act involves great

emotional risk. As an artist you have taken something from deep within yourself and placed it out for the world to see. You have exercised an act of courage, putting forth a part of your heart – something invested with your fondest hopes – and given it the best of which you are capable. You have laid it out, innocent and vulnerable, hoping that it will be loved in the same measure as the love with which it was created. It is new, fresh, and filled with bright hope – unprepared for the bright sunlight of harsh scrutiny.

When it is rejected – and this rejection can come as a rebuke by someone of professional significance, or the merest glance or lack of enthusiasm by someone you love and trust – there is a feeling of desolation that can cut to the very core of your being. How deep it runs, and how fully it overwhelms you, depends on your own emotional make-up and confidence in the strength of your own vision.

I cannot tell you how to respond to rejection; I can only tell you that it will come, that you must be prepared to deal with it, and that you must not let it defeat you.

What you must do is find a way to allow yourself to grieve appropriately and in sufficient measure to be able to move forward without carrying unhealed wounds that skew your vision and cloud your judgment.

Make no mistake, rejection is a wound. And a wound unhealed, like an anger unresolved, festers below the surface, causing us to lose the emotional balance necessary to move forward with grace and confidence. We begin to harbour grudges, to see conspiracies against us, to feel persecuted and misunderstood. We turn against the very world that our creative spirit asks us to embrace.

Such attitudes are poison to our art. How can we feel the freedom to create if we fear the judgment of those around us? How can we keep ourselves open to the richness of human experience if we harbour a grudge against any who might choose to reject us? Remember, your feeling of rejection is greater than the investment of those who have rejected you. Allowing their rejection to claim you gives them and their point of view power over you, and you should never give anyone power over your creative vision. You cannot know whether their rejection is because they understand your work better than you do or because they don't understand it at all.

The world is full of people who want to see others fail – people who are blind to their own motives and who act from petty jealousy or unexamined insecurity. The opinions of these people matter, as the opinions of all people matter, because they are the responses of people you were hoping to reach with your work. But they are not necessarily the sharp edge of truth, and you must not take them as truth any more than you should take the words of those who praise you as truth.

Let the praise of others buoy you, but do not let the attacks of others destroy you. Most of all, seek the voices of those who can teach you. Their words will shine light onto your art and move your creative vision forward.

Keep in mind that rejection is not the same as failure. Rejection merely means that someone, rightly or wrongly, did not find value in your work. It could happen because what you do did not meet their emotional or intellectual needs; it could come because they did not see clearly what you were attempting; it could come because they were having a bad day and were not emotionally present to your work. It can have any of a hundred sources. Failure only comes when you allow rejection to defeat you. And this is something you should never allow to happen.

Remember that in choosing to create you have acted with a rare courage. You have let down the mask; you have called forth your best self; you have taken a chance and revealed your heart to the world. This, no matter how struggling and unformed the creation it brings forth, is a praiseworthy act. For all creation is an act of love, and in the merest making of your art you have, in your own small way, made the world a little richer, a little warmer, and a little more filled with love.

And for that you need feel no shame and make no apology, no matter what others say about your work.

9

The Merchants of Doubt

The harsh reality of critics and criticism

'By plucking her petals, you do not
gather the beauty of the flower.'
Rabindranath Tagore

A TRUE STORY.

It was early in my writing career, and I was not yet acquainted with the world of critics and criticism. I had written a heartfelt book of thoughts for my young son – what I wanted him to know about life if I should die before he reached adulthood. It was the purest book I could write in the most honest way that I could write it. It was filled with love.

Shortly after its publication I received a call from a major national magazine. They were doing an issue for Father's Day and wanted to interview me about the book. I was ecstatic.

A few days later their reviewer called and we talked for almost an hour. It was a warm conversation, filled with shared reminiscences and personal anecdotes about what it meant to be a father. At the end of the interview he thanked me for my time and we each went our separate ways.

I could hardly contain myself. Someone had understood my work and was going to help me share it with the world.

Several weeks later, as Father's Day approached, I was in Chicago doing a series of readings. But my mind was on the review that was scheduled to come out in that national magazine. Like a child waiting for Christmas I went to the newsstands and kiosks on almost an hourly basis, asking if the new edition had arrived. Finally, one man dug through his pile of morning deliveries and pulled out a fresh copy.

I fairly grabbed it from his hands and, without even waiting to get off the street corner, dug into its pages, expecting to find a warm rehash of the conversation the reviewer and I had shared, filled with his insights about the book and praise for the gift I had created for my son. But what I found was a one-sentence reference in a larger article dismissing my work as 'pop psychology and greeting card sentimentalism'.

I was devastated. How could this reviewer have seen pop psychology and greeting card sentimentalism in so carefully crafted a book from the heart of a father? How could he have reduced the insights of my twenty years of training in religion and hard struggles at spiritual formation to 'aphoristic advice'? Most of all, how could he have betrayed the trust and exploited the intimacy of our hour of conversation to produce something so steeped in cruelty and disdain?

I was so upset that I sat down to write a response, until a friend convinced me to hold back. 'Get used to it,' he said. 'He was just doing his job.'

And he was right. That I did not like what the reviewer had said did not matter. He had been exercising his right and responsibility as a critic to assess and pass judgment on my work.

In truth, he was a bad critic. He did not try to illuminate what I had done, which is what a good critic should do. He just smashed it with a literary hammer. And he did so with apparent glee.

Such cruel assessments happen. Critics, like people in all occupations, come in different shapes and sizes.

If your work achieves any sort of public presence, you will feel the outsized effect of criticism. It will not always be a pleasant experience.

But here is what you must keep uppermost in your mind: critics, by the very nature of their task, must stand on the outside of the creation. They do not – indeed, they cannot – look upon your work for what it really is: an act of love.

They do not see that each line written, each phrase shaped, each stroke on the canvas, is, in the moment of its making, a great affirmation, a great and coura-geous 'Yes!' It is you taking a leap of faith and saying, 'Of all the choices I could have made, I chose you.' It is a statement of belief made real.

Criticism cannot understand this because it is not born of love, it is born of analysis, even if it is compas-sionate analysis. Just as someone who is not a parent can appreciate but never truly understand the love you feel for a child, a critic who is not an artist can never truly understand the love you have for your work. They will forever be on the outside, and can never hope to do more than look upon your relationship with compassion and sympathy.

That having been said, it is important to keep in mind that not all criticism is bad.

Good criticism – the deft touch that moves your work in a new and unexpected direction – is a gift to be sought and treasured. It does not demean you; it teaches you and enlightens you. It places your work in a larger context and reveals it from points of view that you may not have considered. The slight pain that it causes you is only the momentary shock of realisation that there was another perspective from which your art could be understood, and that this other perspective has something to offer.

It is bad criticism – the kind that hurts and kills – that is to be avoided. It can be recognised by its failure to see any good in your work or to give you any guidance that allows you to move further along your path as an artist. It has an anger and mean-spiritedness in it. It judges rather than teaches.

But even at its best, criticism is dangerous, at least when you are in the middle of the process of artistic creation. When you create, you must necessarily be inside your work. You cannot afford to have a critical voice whispering in your ear, whether that voice is your own or the voice of an outside observer.

Criticism may be useful in helping you understand what you have done after you have done it, but it is seldom helpful in guiding your hand or heart in the actual act of creation. In that moment you must be in love with your choices and making them with the confidence and courage that all love demands.

It is crucial that you understand this. If your work ever gets a public face, it will draw responses from others. Some of those responses will be positive, some will be harsh. But they must forever be kept at a distance from the actual act of creation, where you must, by necessity, be hearing the clear, small magical voice that says, in the words of Molly Bloom in the last sentence of James Joyce's *Ulysses*, 'yes I will Yes'.

The critical voice will, at worst, cause you to say, 'No,' and at best to say 'Maybe.'

Those are voices that, in the magical and fragile moment of creation, you must not allow yourself to hear.

10

The Dark Companion

The toll of money on the creative spirit

'The arts are not a way to make a living.
They are . . . a way to make your soul grow'
Kurt Vonnegut

'The soul of the artist is oppressed by the
atmosphere of the counting house.'
Franz von Dingelstedt

BILLS ARE CONSISTENT. Income is not.

There it is. Once you realise the full implications of that simple statement you can begin to deal with the least palatable and most omnipresent reality of a life in the arts: the tyranny of money.

Money is a burden for everyone, because money, though not our reason for living, is at the centre of our lives. But money is an especially onerous burden for the artist, because what is at the centre of our life controls our consciousness, and, for an artist, our consciousness and our ability to direct it is the source of our creative power.

We don't go into the arts because we want to make money. We go into the arts because we want to create.

It seems unfair that we must spend our lives foraging for the finances necessary to make those creations. But that is how it is, because the arts, no matter what the discipline, are project-based; when you have finished a project, you find yourself exhilarated, spent, and without work. So, with rare exceptions, artists are always worried about where the next job, and the accompanying income, will come from.

Unless you are independently wealthy or one of the rare few who achieves financial security through the practice of your art, you must make a hard choice when it comes to money. Either you can take jobs related to your art to keep your heart close to the art you love, but risk dissipating your creative energy in creating works of inconsequence; or you can protect your creative energies by making a living doing something completely unrelated to your art, but risk losing connection with the art in your heart.

Artists at all times have struggled with this, and artists at all times have chosen each of these routes. Which route you choose will depend a great deal on your temperament and inner strength.

Let me tell you a story from my own life.

I had finished my formal artistic training and was set to embark upon what I hoped would be a long and meaningful career sculpting life-sized figures in wood. I had drunk at the font of Michelangelo, Donatello and Rodin, and though I knew my work could never achieve the quality of their creations, I could use them as a measure of my dreams. As Michelangelo himself had said, 'He who fights with nobodies wins nothing.' I had no interest in fighting with nobodies. I wanted to wrestle with angels. I wanted to dance with the gods.

But, like everyone else who weds himself to the arts, I soon found out that the world had its own demands. Bills were piling up; rent was coming due. I could apply for all the grants I wanted, enter all the competitions for commissions I could find, but nothing was going to stop the inexorable march of financial obligations that were closing in around me.

I weighed my options carefully. If I stayed close to my art – carving door lintels, signs for restaurants and the like – I would keep my hands and eye active, and the quality of my craft would increase. But I would run the risk of dissipating my creative energy on mind-numbing inconsequential projects.

If, on the other hand, I devoted myself to something completely unrelated to my art, I would protect my creative energy but would be kept at a far remove from the art form that I dearly loved and so desperately sought to pursue.

At that particular time I was eking out a marginal living by producing 'jolly monk on the end of a wine barrel' carvings for a local wine distributor. I had reduced the design to its simplest form and had become proficient at turning out smiling monks with a minimum of effort.

But I was feeling like an artistic charlatan. The barrel ends meant nothing to me, the carvings did not engage me. My success was in efficiency, not in the quality of my vision. I felt my creative energies slipping away; I had become a slave to the mercantile and banal.

And so, in a desperate effort to reclaim my creative

vibrancy, I decided to go in the complete opposite direction. I took a job driving a cab.

I chose the night shift – driving from four or five in the evening to six or seven in the morning – because I believed that with a few hours' sleep at the end of my shift I could still have the better part of every day to work on my sculpture.

Gone would be the mind-numbing, soul-deadening days of incising jolly monks on the ends of wine barrels. Instead, I would be immersed in the heart-quickening but spiritually animating chaos of city traffic, and the crazy, unpredictable *mélange* of humanity that climbs into the cab in the course of an urban night. When daylight came, I would be in my studio, shaping images that corresponded not to the requirements of some alcohol distributor, but to the shape of my vision and dreams.

And so began this new phase of my artistic life.

Each day, as the afternoon waned, I would gather in the dingy, greasy stench of the cavernous cab garage with the other night-shift drivers. We would stand around like day labourers, waiting for our cab assignments and sharing tales of fares we had picked up the night before.

Some drivers drank furtively from whisky bottles they kept in their coats. Some popped pills and smoked cigarettes. Some sat alone in corners reading paperback novels or working crossword puzzles. I occupied myself with visions of the sculpture I would be working on when the shift was through.

When, at last, my number was called and I was assigned my vehicle, I would clean out the overflowing ashtrays and wipe the slime off the seats, then make my way out of the darkened confines of the cab garage into the din and glare of the rush-hour afternoon to begin my twelve-hour shift behind the wheel.

Within moments my entire consciousness would change. The dispatcher barked rapid-fire addresses through the cab radio. Traffic surged and stalled as drivers cut in front of me and raced to beat red lights. My whole body tensed and my attention heightened. The collective anger that is urban rush-hour traffic overwhelmed me.

As twilight descended, the streets would quiet and

the frantic rush-hour crowd would give way to the more leisurely dinner-hour crowd, which would give way to the alcoholics going four blocks to the local bar, which would give way to the decked out party-goers, which would give way to the angry, violent closing-time drunks who urinated sloppily into plastic cups in the back seat, or slapped their girlfriends, or sobbed on my shoulder, or brandished knives and guns, or simply passed out.

Then came the pimps and whores and junkies who wore sunglasses at three in the morning, interspersed with the occasional emergency run to the hospital, or the woman who had been abandoned by her date at a party, or the terrified motorist stuck with a flat tyre on the side of some darkened road.

Finally, as morning light began to bleed colour back into the city, the shift would end with the quiet, unseen service workers – the bakers, the domestics, the custo-dians – on their way to prepare the breakfasts and wash the floors and open the shops so the daylight people would step forth from their morning commute into a world that was already fully in operation.

It was the human drama without parallel. The wealthiest, the poorest; people in a hurry, people with nowhere to go; the desperate, the lonely; wedding parties, thieves running from the police, people having fist fights, couples wanting a dark place to make love – they all got into the cab in the course of an ordinary shift. One night I drove seventy miles between hospitals with a Styrofoam package of human eyeballs sitting on the seat beside me.

It was fascinating, exhilarating, terrifying, and exhausting.

When, at the end of my shift, I pulled my cab back into the garage and turned my keys over to the day driver, I was emotionally spent and spiritually drained. The images of the night swirled around me and tore at my mind and my heart.

Later that day, when I would stand before the half-realised sculpture in my studio, trying to read the rhythm of a curve or to anticipate the effect that a particular shadow on an eye would have on the emotions of the viewer, I would find that the cab still owned my consciousness.

My attention kept drifting back to the old woman who had carried her change in a silk coin purse and gone three blocks to the store to buy four cans of tuna and a loaf of white bread as her grocery supplies for the week, or the crazed, rambling man who had demanded that I put a jacket over my microphone so the government couldn't give him subliminal messages through my radio.

Try as I might to be present to the sculpture before me, I could not erase the images and emotions of the night in the cab. My internal rhythms were wrong, my attention span was fractured, my nerve endings were too frayed. The contemplative distance and singularity of focus needed for the long, slow unfolding of a single image was receding from me like a ship disappearing into the mist.

Whether I liked it or not, the sights, sounds, smells, and rhythms of my life in the cab had overtaken me.

Kent Nerburn, the sculptor, had become Kent Nerburn, the cab driver.

I had discovered one of the hard truths of life: you become what you do.

A stronger man than I might have been able to rise above the immediacy of his circumstances. But I could not.

And my situation was not unique. I have an actor friend whose greatest dream is to have significant roles in serious films but has to make his living waiting tables and taking roles as a slow-witted husband in dish detergent commercials. Another friend – a visual artist – supports his dreams of gallery shows and museum exhibitions by working in a shop putting together frames for graduation photos and paintings bought at craft shows. A friend who longs to play Beethoven's string quartets on concert stages has to make ends meet by playing dance tunes at local weddings. And my friends who have taken the worthy route of teaching in hope that the steady pay cheque will allow them to buy some emotional time for their own artistic endeavours have soon found themselves devoting themselves more to the artistry of shaping lives than to the creation of their own art.

Such is the lot of the artist. The demands of making

a living collide with the dreams of the creative life, and too often the dreams of the creative life lose.

This is not to say that it can't be done. William Carlos Williams was a physician and seemed to wear it well as he spent his evenings writing poetry. T.S. Eliot was a banker. Charles Ives and Wallace Stevens were insurance executives. Composer Philip Glass was a plumber. Vivian Maier was a nanny. Kurt Vonnegut sold cars.

These people all managed to produce significant creations while labouring at tasks far removed from the art they loved.

But it is not an easy course.

Just keep in mind that the danger of losing touch with your art is always present if you move too far from the practice of that art. And working at tasks that are tangential to your art can suck the energy from the grand creations that live inside your imagination. But it is also true that earning a living by something far from your art can offer you the freedom to pursue your highest creative vision, if you are strong enough to claim the space and retain the focus to turn the time you have purchased to the pursuit of that vision.

It is always a risk. But in the end you must choose: if your art cannot support your life, your life must support your art.

Whichever road you decide to travel, know that the need to make money will grind on you, pull on you, whisper at you, and pull your mind and heart downward to the harsh realities of economic survival in a world that often thinks that the merest right to practise your art form should be compensation enough.

Early on you should make your peace with the inevitability of this struggle. Accept the fact that in the world of artistic commerce we artists are like farmers. We are the producers, and if our crops are faulty or the market has no interest in them, we shrivel and perish. The people in the middle – the ones who bring them to market – share the risk. But their risk is spread over many of us, and they will ask us to take less for our labours before they will sacrifice their own returns.

It has ever been thus, and it will very likely always

be so. Think about how Vincent van Gogh, one of the great artists in history, managed to survive: he was supported by the finances of his brother, Theo. And what was Theo's skill and occupation that allowed him this financial security? He was a middleman, a broker, a dealer in art.

What you must keep uppermost in mind is that money can't make you happy but poverty can make you miserable. Poverty is a form of hunger, and hunger consumes the spirit. You must find a way to ward off poverty without giving money too much importance. Your wealth is in your talent, your vision, and your dream of artistic creation. Money is only the tool to set that wealth free.

Find a way to keep poverty and her dark companions from sapping your spirit, and you will find that the gift you have been given – the gift of the creative imagination – gives your life a wealth and meaning that no amount of money can buy.

11

The Golden Handcuffs

The tyranny of success and recognition

'Success is more dangerous than failure,
the ripples break over a wider coastline'
Graham Greene

'In most cases, success equals prison'
Henri Matisse

ALL ARTISTS KNOW this: the more success you have, the more the public and those on the financial side of the arts will want you to repeat what you have done before. A painter who wants to change styles is counselled to stay with what works. An actor who has had great success playing a certain type of character is asked again and again to play variations on this same character. And the story is repeated in similar ways throughout the arts.

In some ways this is a great compliment. It means you have developed enough of an artistic identity to have created expectations on the part of your followers. But it also defines the path you are expected to walk. And the essence of true artistic creativity is to be able to explore pathways you have never explored before.

If you are a caring person who has not reduced your supporters to an abstract concept of audience, this places you in a difficult situation. You wish to explore new realms, and you wish to bring your followers along on these explorations. But you don't want to lose them on the journey, for it is their interest in your work that has helped it come alive, and it is their support that keeps you afloat financially to continue to do the work that they value.

Still, you know you cannot allow them to define who you are and what you do. After all, it was the quality and uniqueness of what you do that made them appreciate your work in the first place. But as a person who must live in this world where money is absolutely crucial to survival, you know that you must listen to the marketplace and to those who guide you through its turns and snares so that you can continue to create without the heavy weight of poverty controlling your mind and burdening your spirit.

The hard truth is that only the truly anonymous

and the independently wealthy have the freedom to create exactly what they wish. The rest of us are, to a great extent, at the mercy of the marketplace, and the marketplace is not about art, it is about solvency.

A friend of mine who works for a large publishing house is fond of saying, 'Writing is an art. Publishing is a business.' The same could be said of the visual arts, or music or dance or any of the myriad art forms that people practise to give voice to the power of the imagination.

There are the creators, and there are the distributors – the people who get the creators known and place their work before the public. If you are intent upon making a living through your art, it is the distributors – those who control the business aspect – who have the power over your work.

If the task of the artist is to take risk, the task of those who bring the art before the public is to manage risk. The concert promoter must sell tickets, the publisher must sell books, the gallery owner must sell art, the theatre manager must fill seats.

We artists live by our imaginations; we don't want

to have to live by the marketplace. We find ourselves frustrated at being commodified for the sake of public consumption. But the fact is, we are commodities to those who bring the art before the public. This does not mean they don't love art or respect our work; it means they look at it differently. Actors groan when they see *Arsenic and Old Lace* or *The Mousetrap* on the docket for the upcoming community theatre season. Musicians do the same when they see *1812 Overture* or *Pictures at an Exhibition* on their list of upcoming concerts. The artists want to touch souls and explore the outer reaches of their creativity, but the business people know they have to pay the bills.

It is hard to reconcile the wings of the imagination with the practical demands of the marketplace. As an artist you want to continue to grow and discover the unexpected. The public, by and large, wants a reprise of the expected.

If you have had a signature hit song, concert-goers will be antsy and fidgeting until they hear those first familiar chords of the song they are anticipating. If, as an actor, you have always played light, comedic characters, your audience will resist and withhold judgment when they see you step on the stage in a Shakespearean role that is filled with pathos and gravity. And the better known you are, the more their expectations calcify and the more your artistic identity is reified in their minds.

As an artist, there is a great asymmetry between you and your audience. You have laid yourself open before them. You have let them take you into their lives. Yet they are in no way a part of yours. You may appreciate them collectively, but you do not know them individually; they, however, feel they have a deeply personal relationship with you. They talk about you, they discuss you, they call you by your first name. You are their personal friend. Their feeling of betrayal is great when you show up as someone they do not recognise. You have walked through the door of their heart and said, 'I'm not who you think I am. I am somebody else.'

Walt Whitman, the great American poet, once said, 'Do I contradict myself? Very well, then I contradict myself; I am large – I contain multitudes.' This is true for all of us, and artists no less than anyone else. But as an artist your identity is reified in the public mind, and those who take care of the business aspect of your career count on that reified identity to promote you and sell you.

You may chafe at this, and believe that those who love your art will follow you wherever you go. For a rare few this is true. But for most of us it is not. If you truly want the freedom to go wherever you wish artistically, your greatest friend is anonymity.

The best time to explore the full range of possibilities in your art form is when you are young and unknown. Sing opera and rock, play bluegrass and classical, do paintings both figurative and abstract.

Establish the base of your identity as broadly as possible. Resist the temptation to focus on what people like and instead do what you like. Once the marketplace chooses something of yours to raise up, you will find yourself defined by the outside world in a way you had never expected. Your dream of being discovered will become the burden of being defined. It is a surprising shift, and when it takes place it has a momentum of its own.

Remember this: the greater your success, the greater the forces that will try to confine you. Though people will become hungrier for your work, they will become very much more specific in what they expect that work to be. And those that help you get your work before the public will become all the more insistent that you give the public what they have come to expect. You will find yourself wearing the golden handcuffs of artistic success.

Though we should all wish to have such concerns, it is a concern nonetheless. You would be wise to prepare for it by keeping your artistic interests as wide and diverse as possible. Then, when the constraining forces of the marketplace try to put artistic shackles on you, though you may not be able to say, 'I am large – I contain multitudes,' perhaps you can say, 'I am large enough that I contain more than one thing.' And those shackles, though still present, will fit more loosely.

THE HIDDEN
SECRETS

12

The Divine Thread

The psychic connection between artist and audience

'Art is not a handicraft, it is the transmission of feeling the artist has experienced.'
Leo Tolstoy

'A real work of art destroys, in the consciousness of the receiver, the separation between himself and the artist.'
Leo Tolstoy

SEVERAL YEARS AGO I was having a conversation with an actor friend over a late night dinner. I was carrying on about some subject that seemed significant to me when suddenly I lost my train of thought.

'I'm sorry,' I said. 'I forgot what I was saying.'

'I know,' he replied.

'What do you mean?' I asked. 'How could you know?'

'Because I wasn't listening,' he said.

In this simple statement lay a truth that every artist knows and every aspiring artist needs to learn: there is a psychic connection between the artist and the audience that must be courted, protected, and fostered. The artist who loses or abuses or denies that thread risks losing the most precious gift that an artist possesses: the capacity to touch those who encounter his or her art.

The question at heart is whether it is in the hands of the artist or the audience to create and foster this connection. I know from my own work that when I read aloud to an audience, if my mind begins to wander and I find that I am only reading words, not meanings and intentions, I am losing my connection with my audience. They may not notice, or may think that the problem is theirs, but I know in my heart that it is I who have lost them, and not the other way around. It is up to me to reach out and embrace them psychically, if I want them to be fully present to my work.

You can say what you will about creating only for yourself, but this membrane of psychic connection is real.

Consider the work that first ignited your passion to become an artist. If it was an active art form, like dance or theatre, it is very likely that the connection created was because the performance was invested with a spiritual presence that reached out and took you in its grasp.

If it was a passive art form, like a painting or a sculpture, you may safely assume that the work that touched you was fashioned by a creator who was spiritually present to the act of creation.

There are exceptions, and it is not impossible that something in you as the viewer or listener or reader was so ready for what that creation had to offer that it touched you despite a flatness or spiritual deadness in the work itself.

But this is rare. In general, the spiritual presence you feel reflects the spiritual presence invested in the work.

As a creator you must trust this truth. Do not think that artistic cunning or technical mastery is enough. Art, as best practised and understood over the centuries, is a spiritual as much as a technical pursuit.

We may have lost much of our spiritual connection in the modern world, but we must not lose it as creators. We are the caretakers of spiritual authenticity, all the more so in a time when the presence of mystery seems so distant from our ordinary lives.

People long for faith. They long for belief. Many

despair of finding it in churches and mosques and synagogues, not because it is not there to be found but because the voice in which it speaks does not always reach out and touch them in the place where they live.

Art, however, does create this touch. It speaks in different voices, different rhythms, different languages. There is no place in the human heart it cannot reach.

Your art comes from a unique place inside of you. Somewhere, that same unique place is hungering for acknowledgment in the heart of another.

You owe it to yourself, you owe it to your art form, you owe it to that person hungering, unknowing, for your artistic voice, to make your art the most authentic creation of which you are capable.

If money is to come, it will. If success and recognition are to come, they will. The only thing you can control is the purity of spirit with which you create.

Remember, there is a world of people out there who long to create but do not know how. When you create, you are speaking not only to them, but for them. If you speak with anything less than the absolute fullness of your artistic spirit, you are betraying the gift that you have been given.

And it is a gift. We, as creators, are a conduit through which the great mystery of creation flows. We fashion something where before there was nothing; we give shape to the cacophony of human experience and invest it with form and beauty and clarified meaning. People who are touched by our art grasp a divine thread that flows backwards to the creative mystery from which it came.

This may sound mystical, but if you have known that moment when the creative act takes you and lifts you and carries you on the wings of something greater than yourself, you have experienced the gift of being in touch with the great mystery of creation.

Why, if you have been given this gift, and the gift to create this moment in the hearts of others, would you ever do anything less than the best of which your mind and hands and heart are capable?

13

The Hummingbird's Heartbeat

The gossamer line between discovery and mastery

'It is idle, having planted an acorn
in the morning, to expect that afternoon
to sit in the shade of the oak.'
Antoine de Saint-Exupéry

LAST NIGHT I attended the staged reading of a play by a wonderful playwright. A staged reading lives on the margin between a full production and a script read-through. The actors are performing, but the blocking and the sets are minimal. In this case, the performance was strong. The script was good; the actors were excellent. But something was wrong. The production never caught fire.

As I left, I pondered over where that flatness, that lack of life, had come from. Was it from me? Had I failed to be fully present to the work unfolding before me? Was it from the work itself? Was there something subtly inauthentic, something I had failed to notice, in the words that the playwright had crafted? Was it in the spareness of the staging – the absence of a meaningful visual component to what was essentially an extended reading?

All of these were possible, but none of them seemed right.

After a night of reflection, I realised that the problem was in the delivery. It was in the spaces, the pauses between words, the imperceptible beat between passages of dialogue. It was in the moment where the actors were unsure of their lines and had to resort to thought to find them because they did not yet own them as their own.

None of the rest of us could catch this consciously. In real time it was little more than a hummingbird's heartbeat. But we could feel it, just as you feel the coldness in someone you meet who takes a dislike to you but does not show it, or the lack of attention in someone whose mind is elsewhere when you are having a conversation. They may be masterful in their subterfuge, but, somehow, something reveals itself that cannot be hidden. It is there in a thousand micro-scopic cues that lie far beneath the level of the observable or measurable. It has to do with confidence and certitude and quality of presence.

T.S. Eliot gave voice to this, though perhaps with different intention, in his haunting poem 'The Hollow Men':

> *Between the conception*
> *And the creation*
> *Between the emotion*
> *And the response*
> *Falls the Shadow.*

It was the shadow that was keeping that reading from coming alive, and it is the shadow that keeps our art from coming alive when we are not in full ownership of the act of creation.

We need certainty when we deliver a line or place a stroke upon the canvas. Hesitation, lack of conviction, may indeed last only a hummingbird's heartbeat, but it is felt like a drummer's lead beat that does not carry in it the presence of anticipation, even though it strikes exactly on the measure.

This certainty comes only with experience and maturity. It cannot be forced. It comes from a thousand failures and a thousand successes and a thousand moments of getting things exactly right. It comes from an understanding deeper than knowledge.

I once showed a sculpture of mine – perhaps the best I had ever done – to the chief curator of a major museum, hoping he would see the power in my work and give me the imprimatur that would advance my career in the way I so desperately sought. But he did not see what I saw, or, if he did, he saw something at once more and less. He saw lack of maturity and lack of resolved certainty.

He saw a work that, though it might be brilliant in the moment (which I felt it was), was brilliant by accident, not by awareness and mastery. Perhaps it pointed to a future of vast potential, but that is all it did: point. The realisation of that vast potential, if it was to take place, was in the future, when ownership of that potential was confident and assured, able to be expressed over and over in a hundred ways and a hundred forms.

When we are early in the practice of our art, when we feel we have done excellent work and feel frustrated that others don't recognise it, we need to remember that true mastery lies in a relaxed control that lives beneath and beyond analysis, and that this cannot be rushed or forced. It is like a wine that must be aged so that the brilliance is in the complexity and the undertones, not only in the brightness and singular beauty.

Yes, there is genius that sometimes overrides the need for patience and resolution, but it is possessed by only the blessed few, no matter how much we wish to claim it for ourselves. And even genius gains a patina of nuance and complexity as it ages, so that in retrospect even the Mozarts and Michelangelos and Martha Grahams of the world show a deepening and enriching as their work matures throughout the course of their lives.

But those of us who are not possessed of genius, or only have flashes of brilliance in our work, must be patient in our creation, for the character in our art reveals itself only as character is revealed in the human face – by the passage of time.

In the strange way that the mind glides through associations and analogies, that staged reading made me think of the sculptures of Donatello, one of my favourite artists. Donatello was not the most technically gifted sculptor of the human figure. His knowledge of anatomy was rudimentary; his capacity for gesture still heavily laden with the iconic stiffness of the medieval. But his figures had the magical characteristic of seeming not as if they were expressing an emotion but as if they had arrived at their emotion. They somehow seemed to have an inner past.

This is what was lacking in the production that I saw. The actors did not seem to have arrived at their dialogue, they merely knew it. The history was lacking; the intentionality was lacking; the idea of an inner life that extended far beyond what they were saying was lacking.

This is what artists new to their craft necessarily lack. Their work may have a presence, even a brilliant presence, but it does not seem to come forth from the fullness of a resolved artistic life. It speaks of the brilliance of discovery, not the resolved awareness of conscious choice.

When we are young in our art, this lack of complete ownership of our work is what keeps it from having fullness and resolution. It has the power and excitement of fresh discovery, but it does not have the settled sense that it was the outgrowth of a fuller knowledge. It does not express a past because it does not have a past. And without a past it does not imply a future.

You need make no apology for being young or new in your work. There is magic in the youthful freshness that exists on the edge of risk and discovery. There will come a time when you will look back upon that freshness and long to reclaim it in your work. But while you are in this stage the impatience can be overwhelming.

You want to be recognised for what you know is inside you. You create what you think is excellent work and wonder why others don't see it. Perhaps they are seeing it. But they are seeing it as promise, not as mastery.

You should cherish this time and be wary of those

who would exploit it by putting you forth as a finished and polished creation. You are a chrysalis, still in the process of becoming.

Remember the actors at that staged reading: they, too, were in a process of becoming. Their work was wonderful but not fully owned. They were chasing their creation, not finding it in the fullness of their stored knowledge. That finding will happen with practice, and it will happen as subtly as the change of morning to afternoon. They may not even know when it occurs.

And just as those actors will one day speak the words of the script as if they flow forth from their own understanding, there will come a day when the works you create will come forth with total confidence and trust from the ever-deepening well of your successes and failures and life experience. This is the day you must work toward with patience and faith.

And when it arrives, you will know it, because on that day, between the conception and the creation, between the emotion and the response, there will be no shadow.

14

The Architect
and the Gardener

The magic of accident
and faith in the unknown

'There is always some accident in the best things,
whether thoughts or expressions or deeds.
The memorable thought, the happy expression,
the admirable deed are only partly ours.'
Henry David Thoreau

No matter what your art form, there is a moment in almost every project when you feel that your work has got away from you. The character you are developing seems false. The story you are writing seems flat and uninteresting. All the choices you have made seem wrong-headed or misdirected and you can see no clear path forward. You are lost in a creative wilderness and you don't know how to escape.

All of us have known these moments. They are part of the creative process. But that does not make them easier to endure. To feel a vision turn to dust in your hands is a painful experience, and the doubt that sets in is not subject to rational analysis. Is this the moment, you wonder, when my vision has left me? Is this the time when I took on too much, when I went at things from the wrong direction, when I overreached my own capabilities?

When I have these moments, I take heart in the words of a young actor friend of mine who had just finished working on his first major Hollywood film. He was, quite rightly, in awe of the experience of working with a veteran director and Oscar-winning actors. When I asked him about the most important lesson he had learned during the filming, he didn't hesitate.

'You can't plan for magic,' he said.

Most art begins with a moment of inspiration. Perhaps it is a sound you hear that calls forth an image, or a passing scene in the course of a day that kindles an idea. Perhaps it is a fleeting thought, arising from some forgotten place in your memory. Whatever it is, it evokes an insight that mysteriously coalesces into a vision you think you can give form through your art.

You are excited. You begin to savour the possibilities. Perhaps you sketch. Perhaps you write. Perhaps you pick up your instrument and begin to frame a tune. Perhaps you stand in front of a mirror and begin to develop a character. You take tentative steps while the vision takes a vague but promising shape that calls you to set about the serious work of bringing it to life.

This is a moment of great excitement. You are filled with the optimism of fresh discovery and the confidence of fresh purpose. Even if only vaguely, you see a way to turn your inspiration into a creation.

But at some point, as the actual process of creation progresses, the moment of uncertainty comes. The pieces don't fit together quite the way you had hoped. The plot doesn't unfold quite the way you had wanted. Your choreography feels forced or the notes don't come together in the way you had envisioned. Confidence wavers and the light of your initial vision begins to dim.

This is not a moment to panic or despair. As the French poet Anna de Noailles said, 'It's at midnight that one has to believe in the sun.' But even more, it is when you are in the darkness that the moments of magic can happen because these are the moments when you are freed from the shackles of expectations and set free in the fields of creative discovery.

I have had a bronze figure fail in the casting, resulting in the loss of its arms and legs. In the end, this accident, so devastating at the time, resulted in a sculpture more powerful than the figure I had designed, because the abruptness and naturalness of the fracture gave the fragment an immediacy that the full figure could never have achieved.

I have had characters get away from me in writing, sending my plot in directions that made me despair of all my plans and expectations, only to find in the end that the characters, having wrested the story from me, moved it in directions that were at once richer and more complex than I had ever imagined.

Every artist who has been working long enough to have had successes and failures can tell similar stories. It is in the nature of creation for works to grow and take on lives of their own, often defying the artist's most cherished intentions.

When this happens, you need to have confidence

you are not lost; you are just at the point of new discovery. Your work has climbed out of the shape of your original idea and begun to claim a life of its own.

Einstein put it well when he said, 'No worthy problem is ever solved within the plane of its original conception.'

As a creator, you need to respect, even savour, the magic of accident and care less about what is being lost than what is being born. Remember that any work of art, in its becoming, follows the rules of evolution, not the rules of human construction: every form remakes itself as new information is discovered and internalised. Decisions build upon each other, steps lead to further steps. Soon enough the place of beginning is but a distant memory, and you are wandering into a land where the possibilities are limited only by your courage and talent and imagination.

When I feel myself lost in the midst of a project, I like to remind myself of the separate skills of the architect and the gardener. The architect designs and builds; he knows the desired outcome before he begins. The gardener plants and cultivates, trusting the sun and weather and the vagaries of chance to bring forth a bloom.

As artists, we must learn to be gardeners, not architects. We must seek to cultivate our art, not construct it, giving up our preconceptions and presuppositions to embrace accident and mystery. Let moments of darkness become the seedbed of growth, not occasions of fear.

If you would truly be an artist, you must believe that your art – whether interpretation, object, or performance – is bigger than the idea that gave it birth. The moments when you are feeling most lost are simply the moments when your art is seeking new growth.

Embrace them. Celebrate them. They are the moments of magic when you are most open to creative possibility.

And it is magic, when it occurs, that turns cold idea into living art.

15

The Right Stroke

The fine art of the appropriate choice

*'No steel can pierce the human heart so chillingly
as a period at the right moment.'*
Isaac Babel

*'Art must spring out of the fullness
and richness of life.'*
Willa Cather

THERE IS A story, probably apocryphal, about Leonardo da Vinci, who was legendary for his dilatory habits and slow working pace. He was also known as one of the few Renaissance artists who allowed visitors to watch him while he worked.

One day a visitor came to observe him as he laboured on his painting *The Last Supper* in the refectory of the convent of Santa Maria delle Grazie in Milan. The man remained all day, observing Leonardo on his scaffolding contemplating the painting before him.

At the end of the day, Leonardo had added just one small brushstroke to his work.

When he came down, the man who had been

watching him said, with some disappointment, 'You were up there all day, but only made one stroke.'

Leonardo, as the story goes, gave a knowing smile and responded, 'Yes, but it was the right one.'

This is a wonderful story that resonates on many levels. It speaks of genius, it speaks of patience; it speaks of the idiosyncratic nature of the artist. But what it also speaks of, that we do not so readily notice, is the necessity of choice.

Think about the stroke that Leonardo made, then consider the thousands of strokes he did not make – the 'almosts' and the 'maybes' and the 'should I's?' that he considered and rejected – as he stood on that scaffold, knowing that the decisions he made would stand for generations as a statement of his artistic vision. In the end, he trusted but that single stroke. And that stroke lives, frozen in time, and speaks to us today.

All of us like to believe in that moment of inspiration that gives life to our work, almost as if it comes from a place beyond ourselves. We seek it, we court it, we perform rituals to prepare ourselves and to call forth its arrival.

We seldom stop to think about the incredible wealth of experience that went into that moment of creative confidence; the astonishing number of choices considered and rejected, often unconsciously, as we sought out that perfect gesture or the precise pause – that 'right stroke' – that gave our work its character and life.

This may be the single most important truth that every mature artist knows: that, at its heart, our art is about what we don't put in – what we considered and rejected; the choices withheld in order to illuminate the choices made. The actor knows the pauses that create tension; the musician knows the rests that build poignancy and offer relief; the novelist knows the spaces in conversations; the painter knows the detail that isn't described.

Early in the practice of our art we seldom think of these things. We believe the essence of the art is what is created, not what is left out. But as we get older we discover that it is the absence that takes up the most space, the silence that speaks most loudly and surrounds what is heard with meaning.

The goal of any art is to pare down to the essence. The French writer Antoine de Saint-Exupéry said that true art is achieved not when there is nothing more to be added but when nothing more can be taken away.

If you would grow in your art, you must become attentive to this truth. In some unseen place, your art is about the discipline of knowing what to leave in, what to leave out, what to choose from life's manifold richness, and what to leave behind.

Sometimes, gaining this knowledge is the hardest task of all – harder than learning the craft, harder than shaping your talent. It is about finding the perfect creative moment when the 'less' becomes the 'more'.

I remember being told by an editor that the key to good writing is being willing to 'kill your babies' – rejecting and leaving behind those favourite passages that you love so much that you will bend the rest of your work to fit around them. This is harsh counsel, but it is true: behind every creative act there are a thousand deaths.

What you need to do is make sure that the artistic soil from which you make your choices is as full and rich as possible, so that those choices are informed by the broadest possible experience. This does not mean only artistic experience, it means experience with the fullness of life.

One of the greatest mistakes you can make is to focus completely on your art, believing that shutting out the rest of the world is the best way to achieve a clear artistic vision. It is, in fact, quite the opposite. Curiosity and openness are perhaps your most important artistic tools.

As artists, our approach to life is unique. Apprehension is more important to us than analysis; the senses more important than the intellect. The intellect drops a template of understanding over experience, bending it toward its preconceptions, while the senses walk through the world, absorbing what it offers, asking nothing of it, accepting it for what it is, taking all that it offers as a gift.

A shaft of sunlight, a baby's cry, an aged face glimpsed in an upstairs window, a memory rising up from a forgotten corner of our life; these are the experiences of life unfiltered – accepted, embraced, and taken for what they are, not for what they mean.

If you remain open to them, in some way that is impossible to explain, they will miraculously coalesce into an emotional awareness that will tell you how long to hold that pause in the song, or how that one colour can call forth a feeling on the canvas, or how to shape the gestures of the character you are playing, because they have informed the whole emotional timbre and texture of your life, and the full power of your senses has come down to breathe life into that single moment – that right stroke – of decisive choice. The actual moment of creation, when it comes, is but the final act – the tip of the brush upon the canvas – of this whole lifetime of experience.

This may sound mystical, but it is not. Not all correlations are direct. Ansel Adams expressed it well when he said that 'A great photograph is a full expression of what one feels . . . about life in its entirety'. And the same can be said for any decision any of us makes as we stand before the blank canvas of artistic possibility.

So don't begrudge those experiences that take time away from your art. They are not time wasted. Art is a way of seeing, of apprehending, and it will always be with you, whether you are creating or not. For in the life of the artist there is no unimportant experience because every experience is a moment of fresh sensation. None of us knows which moment will ignite an insight or elicit an understanding that will inspire us or spark our art to life.

When it comes time to make that ultimate act of courage that so few on the outside understand – that single stroke, that single snap of the shutter that you hope will bring your work alive – you can make it with confidence.

And though you may not be able to articulate it in words, when those around you ask how you came to choose that exact gesture, that exact colour, that exact moment to capture the image, you will be able to say, with quiet conviction, 'I cannot tell you how I made that particular choice, but I know in my heart that it was the right one.'

16

Abandoning Your Children

The hard decision to leave works behind

'I don't let myself get carried away by my own ideas; I abandon 19 out of 20 of them every day.'
Gustav Mahler

I RECENTLY SPENT three weeks working on a chapter of a book. I wrestled with it, argued with it, tried entering into it with different voices and from different points of view. But nothing worked. Finally, despite all my investment and all my labours, I had no choice but to acknowledge the hard truth: I walked over to my desk, picked up the reams of false starts and threw them into the waste basket. I abandoned my child.

It was a sad, but not unfamiliar, moment. Some efforts are destined never to rise above the level of rough sketches or explorations. They simply do not have within them the capacity to congeal into a work of art.

That chapter had begun with such high hopes – the concept was good, my voice seemed strong, the words flowed easily. But, try as I might, I could not wrestle it into any sort of literary shape. In the end it remained a fragmentary, recalcitrant, uneasy combination of prose and thought that never could find a meaningful form.

I could have continued to labour it forward. Perhaps I might have been able to finesse it into something of value. But I don't think so. This was just one of those obdurate pieces that was destined to elude me, no matter what efforts I put in to crafting or adjusting or manipulating.

Knowing the difference between what is just resisting your initial efforts and what is essentially a false direction is a skill all artists must acquire. There are false starts aplenty, even in good work. But some efforts are doomed to forever remain in pieces, lacking that aesthetic thread that pulls them into a unified form.

Creating art of any form is always a wager. You are betting that your talent and imagination will pull something out of an initial idea. But all art is exploration, and sometimes exploration does not issue forth in discovery.

I remember one short piece I wrote about a stone I had found in the Arctic. I woke one morning, grabbed a cup of coffee, sat down in my favourite chair and wrote it from beginning to end. There was no labouring and almost no conscious thought. I'm not even sure I had any idea what I was going to write when I sat down that morning. And I love what I produced.

Then there was the instance of a sculpture I did for a monastery in British Columbia. The monks were literal men, strong in the simplicity of their Benedictine faith and quite uninterested in visual metaphor or abstraction. They wanted a representational image of their patron saint, Joseph the Worker, and they wanted it sculpted from a log of local yellow cedar – the same tree spoken of in the Scriptures as the cedars of Lebanon.

Subtractive sculpture – sculpture that is carved rather than built up – is a true test for a visual artist.

You have no eraser; there are no do-overs. Each stroke limits your future options, and the certainty or the lack of clarity of your vision reveals itself stroke by stroke with unerring inevitability.

What was significant about this sculpture was that the right arm emerged from the tree with absolute ease. The gesture was sure; the always difficult junction of the wrist and the forearm fell into place perfectly. It came forth as easily as the essay on the stone in the Arctic, and it possessed confidence, accuracy, and grace.

The left arm, however, fought with me. I miscalculated the gesture, and the relationship of the forearm to the hand was wrong. I laboured diligently, clarifying the musculature of the forearm and the structure of the fingers, getting them as perfect as I could make them. I worked on it for almost three weeks and, in the end, though it was accurate in all its specifics, the overall effect was wrong. The arm had failed at its moment of conception, and all my efforts to adjust and clarify and correct had only served to magnify the wrongness of my initial idea.

Had that arm been an independent free-standing creation, I would have abandoned it and written off the effort as a learning experience. But because it was part of a sculpture that had to be completed, it was and remains the physical embodiment of the wrongness of an ill-conceived artistic effort – an artefactual documentation, along with the right arm, of the possibility of creation with easy grace and the sad truth of the futility of laboured effort on a flawed idea.

There is a lesson in this for all artists in all genres: you must learn to make peace with creations and artistic ideas that will never rise above the level of sketch or study.

Some of the best writing I have ever done lies in drawers and files and waste bins — fragmentary echoes of ideas that could never find a worthy literary shape. Every musician I know has musical sketches and phrases that lurk forever in the back of the mind. Actors try a hundred ways of interpreting a character, discarding almost all of them before settling on a single interpretation.

All the false attempts and missteps are but the

unfortunate collateral damage of the search for a final artistic form. They are the abandoned artistic children left on the side of the road.

But think hard before you abandon these works completely. Sometimes they are not fundamentally flawed, but merely wrong for the moment.

I have an artist friend who contends that you should never throw anything away. Everything has its time, he says, and just because a work refuses to take form at a given moment does not mean it will not someday come to life.

Other artists say that any idea that refuses to take form has missed its moment and should be abandoned for good. In their minds, to bring it back at a later date is to attempt to reclaim something that has lost its savour, or never had any savour from the beginning.

It has worked both ways for me. As a writer, very seldom has a fully formed passage that I abandoned found a place in a subsequent creation. To make it fit in a new iteration would require wedging a discrete creation into a different work with a very separate voice and rhythm and flow, and that seldom happens.

But some works that never got beyond the stage of a rough sketch have become the seedbeds of future creations. They were the gathering of a force around an idea that I found significant. That they did not find an appropriate form does not mean that the idea that gave them birth was faulty. Perhaps, as my friend says, their time simply had not come.

The creative process is a mysterious thing. It defies the rational and confounds the rules of logic. Sometimes answers come by hard labour, other times by unexpected epiphany. Sometimes no answers are forthcoming at all, and your creative efforts end up on the scrapheap of your imagination, where you glance at them occasionally, wondering if you should have approached them differently or if, under the right circumstances, they could have had a productive creative life.

Just know that you need have no regrets about your decision to abandon those works that will not come into form. Far more damage comes by pushing a flawed idea to a forced conclusion than by letting it pass and turning your attention to more promising or fruitful avenues of enquiry.

All work nourishes the soil of your creative imagination. And all work increases your understanding of your craft. Sometimes a work takes flower, sometimes it merely enriches the soil. And sometimes the seed of an idea, long abandoned and even forgotten, emerges suddenly in a place where it was least expected. And sometimes the blooms that it produces are the most beautiful of all.

17

Time and Timing

The art inside your art

'Art is never finished, only abandoned.'
Leonardo da Vinci

'Patience is also a form of action.'
Auguste Rodin

KNOWING WHEN TO stop, when to continue, how to bring your work to completion without losing your creative energy – these are challenges all artists face, and how you deal with them will determine much about the quality of your work and the way you feel about what you have accomplished.

We have all heard the famous canard spoken by Leonardo da Vinci and echoed by so many others, that a work of art is never finished, only abandoned. In our minds we know this is true, but it is hard to accept in our hearts. When we have laboured long on a project and have watched it move ever closer to what we want it to be, we don't want to give up on it until we craft it to perfection.

'Just a little more,' we say. 'Just a little adjustment and I'll have it.'

Soon enough it overtakes us. We go from joyful preoccupation to creative obsession. We can't sleep, we can't get it out of our mind. The world has fallen away and nothing else matters. Our artistic child is crying out to be born.

Every artist knows this feeling, whether it is the actor trying to shape a character, the composer trying to get the orchestration just right, the writer trying to expand a description, or the painter trying to decide whether to add another colour to the canvas. We are seeking that moment when our work turns toward us and says, 'I am complete. I am done. I am all I ever can be.'

In truth, this seldom happens. More often we reach a point where we become blind to our work. We find ourselves analysing rather than creating, hoping that by parsing our decisions one more time or a little more closely we will come to some certainty and clarity, when in fact, with each parsing, we are becoming less clear and less certain. We know too much and trust too little. Eventually, we reach a point when we simply have to say, 'Enough. I choose to let go.'

This is a difficult moment, because letting go is an act of faith, not an act of knowledge. It is a moment when courage meets instinct and we have to choose, against what feels like our better judgment, to step back and set the work free.

Knowing how to choose this moment is an art in itself, because no matter how good we get technically or how confident we become in our creative process, indecision is always present. And you will never know if your work is less than it could have been if you had quit a day sooner or gone on a day longer.

I cannot tell you how to choose this moment. I can tell you that it ultimately comes down to trusting a feeling, and that you gain more confidence in that feeling the longer you work in your art.

I can also tell you that overworking your art is a greater danger, especially for a beginning artist, than letting go too soon. Overworked art is tired art, while freshness has a power, even if a work is imperfect or incomplete. Better to have a work that has the rough edges of spontaneity than a work that has no edges at all. Or, as Lao Tzu, the Taoist sage, put it, 'Keep sharpening your knife and it will blunt.'

Having said all this, knowing when to make the decision remains a leap of faith. But make it you must, because if you fail to make it, you either labour your work to death or never finish anything. Neither is a worthy outcome for all the effort you have put into your art.

There is another issue of timing that challenges us in an even more insidious way. It comes on subtly, almost unnoticed, like the changing of the tides or the turning of the seasons. It happens like this: you have laboured on your work with single-minded intensity, entering into it every day with all the artistic energy at your command. You try on one idea after another. You winnow the choices before you little by little, searching for that one moment when the 'less' becomes the 'more'. You are fascinated with its possibilities and driven by the vision of what the work might yet be. It is at the centre of your life.

Then one day, for no apparent reason, you wake up and find yourself oddly uninterested in the task. You feel distracted, almost disengaged. You have no focus; your mind begins to wander. Other artistic projects begin to creep into your thoughts. The work you once wore like a second skin seems somehow distant and uninvolving. You have come to one of the artist's other most feared moments: you are done, but the work is not finished.

Unlike the dilemma of not knowing when your work is complete, you now wonder if you will be able to complete it at all. You have become immobilised not by confusion but by indifference.

Though these would seem to be almost opposite emotional conditions, they are both expressions of a similar creative malady: you are spiritually exhausted. You have allowed your artistic preoccupation to overtake you, and your work is gasping for air.

The first instinct when you encounter these creative impasses is to try to push past them. 'Work harder,' you tell yourself. 'Stay the course. This is a failure of discipline on my part.'

But discipline is not always an antidote to spiritual exhaustion. There are times when stepping back and letting your work breathe is the best thing you can do.

The words of the Tao Te Ching speak clearly about this matter: 'Trying to grasp things, you lose them. Forcing a project to completion, you ruin what was almost ripe.'

You don't want to ruin your work by forcing it to an untimely completion, just as you don't want to ruin your work by labouring it to death or abandoning it too soon. You want it to ripen in the fullness of its own time. A creation, after all, is a birth. You can't force that birth by ceaseless effort.

None of us knows the exact moment when our creation wants to be born and none of us knows the process by which it arrives at that moment. From the first second of its conception, it has been struggling to get free from you and to take on a life of its own.

The Taoists have another saying that is also well worth considering. 'Love', they say, 'is creating without owning.'

If you truly love your work, you must learn to create

it without owning it. You must learn not to confuse your preoccupation with bringing it to life and the natural ripening process of the creation itself.

When you feel you have lost touch with your work or your work has lost touch with you, it merely means you have gotten out of step with the natural rhythms of its creation. It wants to breathe, but you are smothering it with your labours and your love.

This is the moment when you need to take a step back. All decisions seem ever more critical as a work nears completion because the weight of finality hangs over every choice. But the truth is that when you have reached this stage, the great mass of your work is already done. Your creation is no longer seeking form, it is seeking clarity.

What you need now is the discipline of patience, not the discipline to work harder or longer. A work needs to relax toward finality. It cannot be pushed, it cannot be worried, it cannot be analysed to completion. Pushing against the natural rhythms of creation will just churn up the waters. Clarity comes only when the waters settle and the air clears.

There are times when the most productive act is to do nothing. This is one of them. You need to step back, let your work breathe; to watch it rather than try to control it. Let it recede from you until you can admire it for what it is rather than worrying about what you think it yet could be.

You have not lost it and it has not escaped from you. You are just looking at it too closely and trying to hold it too tightly. Let it fly free.

Soon enough, at a time of its own choosing, like a wandering child, it will return to its origins and show itself to you anew.

Then, seeing it clearly once again, you will be able to guide it safely home.

THE UNSEEN
JOYS

18

Many Hands
and a Common Heart

The joys and challenges of collaboration

*'The deepest level of communication is not
communication, but communion.'*
Thomas Merton

*'When you are playing with someone who really
has something to say, even though they may be
otherwise quite different in style, there's one thing
that remains constant. And that is the tension of
the experience, that electricity, that kind of feeling
that is a lift sort of feeling.'*
John Coltrane

WHO AMONG US has not been to a play or a concert where suddenly the entire energy of the room aligns; when what moments before was a group of appreciative and attentive individuals transforms, as if by magic, into a single heart beating as one with the event taking place before them? Such moments of creative alchemy are a joy for an audience, but they are the absolute lifeblood of the artist.

I still remember when, as a young boy of seventeen, I snuck into a smoky nightclub to hear Muddy Waters and Little Walter play. The musical union they achieved was so magical that I have never forgotten it. It was conversation, it was argument, it was complicated discussion. It was filled with humour and danger and intimacy. It was two men in total control of their instruments and so in tune with each other musically and emotionally that merely to witness it felt like a gift.

Muddy Waters and Little Walter played thousands of concerts with countless musicians over the years, and I'm sure that the music they created often rose to a magical level. But no other pairing at no other time could have created what I witnessed that night. It is not too much to say that it was a musical act of love.

If you are an artist who works with others – a musician, an actor, a dancer – you may well know these experiences. And, if you do, you know that you live for these transformational moments when talents merge and something is created that is greater than anything you could ever create alone.

It is the artistic equivalent of the creation of a child. Like a child, it is alive, and, like a child, it is both a part of and apart from those who created it. This is why performing with others is so intoxicating. When all else is stripped away, those elusive moments of almost mystical artistic connection are nothing short of a spiritual union.

But with this intimacy comes danger. Just as more than one voice is needed to create artistic harmony, different voices working together also run the risk of artistic discord and dissonance. Egos get in the way. Differences of talent and interpretation surface. Artistic unions come apart as surely as they came together. When this happens, feelings of anger, even betrayal, arise.

This is not difficult to understand. Blending yourself with another in any aspect of life requires a great deal of trust. You make yourself vulnerable. You submerge your personal needs into a larger whole in the hope of creating something that transcends you both. You risk everything for the sake of the common good.

When this trust is violated, the feeling of betrayal is equal in proportion to the amount of trust that was given. This is why the acrimony of musical groups that fall apart or the bitterness of actors who harbour great grudges against other actors or directors appear so outsized in relation to the differences that caused the feuding. On the surface it seems like a clash of egos, but often it is the result of something far softer and more human: the response to a trust betrayed.

Artistic creation has, by its very nature, a profoundly self-protective component. You have sacrificed everything to become impeccable in your craft. You have had to make choices and defend choices and hold firm against voices that have criticised you and challenged you and belittled your goals. You have staked your artistic integrity and self-worth on the creations you have made and the artist you have become.

When someone tries to dominate that or change that or twist it to their own ends, you fight against it like a parent fights against the harming of a child. Yet, if you find your way through these difficulties, you have a chance to experience something with others that those of us in solitary art forms seldom know.

As a practitioner of one of those solitary art forms, I have little opportunity to work with other artists. But I have had glimpses of the magic that happens when you merge individual talents in a collective work of art.

A musician friend once proposed that he and I give a performance that combined my reading with his playing. Our temperaments, as well as our arts, could hardly have been more different. He's a man of the sunlight; I'm a man of the shadows. I seek to console; he speaks to inspire. His work brings people together; mine sends them into themselves.

By all accounts, the two of us should have had no grounds for working together successfully, but because we honoured our differences and protected the gossamer thread of trust between us, all involved got more than they expected. The audience got both celebration and reflection. My friend experienced a level of *gravitas* he seldom knew in his performances, and I was participant in a moment of artistic joy that I had never known in my time of solitary readings and public presentations. We are anxious to work together again.

Imagine, then, the pleasure experienced by a thoughtful, reflective cellist in musical conversation with a gregarious, optimistic pianist. Or a ballerina of unsurpassing delicacy and lyricism dancing with a male partner whose artistic voice is grounded in muscularity. If they grant each other the integrity of their individual aesthetics, together they can achieve something that neither of them could achieve alone. They may even surprise each other and find that each brings forth from the other something that neither knew even existed.

The key is in having mutual artistic respect. All art reflects countless hours of practice and searching and decision-making, as well as the unique temperament of the individual artist. How can you not respect the talent of someone who has travelled that hard road, even if you do not like their personality or do not agree with their aesthetic choices? They, like you, are an artist, and they, like you, deserve respect for what they have accomplished.

Not all artists are pleasant human beings. I have a composer friend who once advised me that there are some who are like batteries: they cannot produce energy unless they are filled with acid. Let these people be who they are, he said. Keep your distance from them if you must, but honour them for what they create.

His counsel is worth taking. In the final analysis, it is the creation that matters. And though all collective creations reflect on some level the chemistry and symbiosis of the artists involved, there is such a thing as transformational magic. Ill-suited partners can create wonderful children.

Egotistical fellow musicians, dictatorial directors and choreographers, actors who demand the stage or the spotlight – these are occupational hazards for those of us who would work on common creations. But intimate musical conversations, directors and choreographers who surprise us with their unexpected brilliance, and actors who bring life to everyone else onstage, are every bit as frequent, and these are the occupational joys.

If, as an artist, you find yourself in a situation of being able to make art with others, treat it with respect, even reverence. It may not rise to the level of magic – it may not even become familial – but if you have patience, and if all the artistic stars are aligned, you may, if only for an instant, see through to that moment when working together can unashamedly be called an act of love.

19

The Solace
of Unlikely Friends

The wisdom and insight of other arts

*'A man should hear a little music, read a little
poetry and see a fine picture every day of his life,
in order that worldly cares may not obliterate
the sense of the beautiful which God has
implanted in the human soul.'*
Johann Wolfgang von Goethe

'A picture is a poem without words'
Horace

WHEN DIFFICULT TIMES come and we find ourselves troubled by indecision and uncertainty about our work, there is much to be gained by placing ourselves in the presence of other art. These works can remind us of why we create, and reconnect us with the source of our creative vision. They provide us with the inspiration and encouragement to return to the fold of the creators with renewed energy and hope.

I recently attended a performance of Mozart's *Requiem*. I was at an impasse in my writing. I was overthinking everything, analysing when I should have been creating, doubting every sentence and every thought. I had killed the rhythm of my work and drained it of all spontaneity and passion.

As I sat in the darkened confines of the concert hall, listening to the voices of the singers layer themselves upward in a kind of choral dance of praise and supplication, the tangle inside my mind began to loosen. I began to breathe ideas rather than think them. Thoughts flowed out of me with an ease and grace that had been eluding me for days. I was inside the music and the music was inside me. It was at once a filling and an emptying, a cleansing and an inspiring. By opening my heart the music clarified my mind.

This is what music does to me. Though I was trained as a sculptor and make my living as a writer, music, for me, has always been the mother art. It carries within it all the values that govern the shaping of my work – rhythm, tempo, line, shape, mass, texture, shading, timbre – and it opens my heart and fills me with creative insight like no other art form.

Oftentimes I don't even realise what I am experiencing. When I listen to Pablo Casals play Bach's unaccompanied cello suites, though I go to the music for its sheer beauty, the poetry of the melodic lines soon overtakes me and I find myself soaring on the music as if on the wind, and I am inspired to reach for the same poetry inside the language of my own prose.

In the same way, Ralph Vaughan Williams' pastoral works fill me with their lyricism and help shape the rhythms and pacing of my writing. Leonard Cohen inspires me with the elegance of his metaphors. Miles Davis teaches me about economy of line. When I hear the Walter Hawkins singers perform 'Goin' Up Yonder' I am carried to a place of joyous faith that reminds me that there are worlds and experiences that are beyond my understanding. And Mahler's spiritual yearning opens my heart and gives me the courage to reveal parts of myself that would otherwise remain hidden.

These are more than simple lessons and inspirations. They are illuminations. They don't inform me, they touch me. They light up my work from within.

And though music is the art form that touches me most deeply, other arts illuminate my work as well.

I know little about the nuances of photography. A beautiful scene, well-composed, or an image offering a poignant window into another reality are enough to satisfy me. But when I stand before a photograph shaped by the hand of Ansel Adams, I experience the magic of a work that contains both immediacy and eternity. Though I cannot apply this directly to my own work, I suddenly apprehend it as an artistic possibility, and it both deepens and broadens the range of my aesthetic understanding.

Likewise, watching the way Akira Kurosawa cuts from scene to scene in his films shows me that juxta-position as well as continuity is a tool of the artist's craft; it inspires me to move from paragraph to para-graph, and even chapter to chapter, without insisting on logical transitions.

These are wonderful experiences, and I value them greatly, but sometimes there is something deeper at work as well. The Germans call it *Einfühlung*, or infeeling – a kind of emotional empathy where a work of art resonates with you so deeply and fundamentally that you identify with it spiritually.

When I first read Rainer Maria Rilke's poem 'The Panther', I found myself carried back to a childhood visit to a local zoo where the animals were kept in small enclosures inside a dank concrete building. Standing at my mother's side amid the reek of disinfectant and the echoing roars of the caged animals, I watched a tiger pace and circle with a frantic intensity until, for an instant, his eye caught mine and I experienced something that will haunt me as long as I live.

That 'something' remained inside of me, dark and unspoken, until I read Rilke's poem and its description of a caged panther – 'the movement of his powerful soft strides is like a ritual dance around a center in which a mighty will stands paralyzed' – and a shiver of recognition ran through me. For the first time, I felt like someone understood what I had experienced. It was as if I was hearing my heart revealed in the words of another. And every time I read that poem that shiver of recognition returns.

In the same way, Frederick Varley's painting *Stormy Weather, Georgian Bay* reaches into me and touches a place that is beyond understanding. As I stand before that painting I feel a knowledge deeper than memory, like I have been in that place at some time I no longer know, staring out from that lonely promontory onto those windswept northern waters. It is as if Varley has painted the contents of my heart. I cannot look at that painting without feeling that someone has understood me at the very core of my being.

Rilke, in his great poem 'Archaic Torso of Apollo', expresses this experience with poetic eloquence when he speaks of standing before that luminous marble fragment with its lifeforce fairly bursting forth from within like the brilliance of a star. 'For here', he says, 'there is no place that does not see you.'

This is what a work of art can do. It can make you feel like it sees you, like it understands you, like it speaks directly to you and your experience. It pierces the fragile shell of the self, and you feel that on some fundamental level not only do you know that work but that work knows you; it comes from a place where your spirit is congruent with the spirit of its creator.

We artists all need to know such works in our lives. They clarify our sense of purpose and remind us of why we create. We can go to them, as to a well, and never drink them dry: we resonate with the spirit that created them, and that spirit is present every time we encounter that work.

You need to find these works in your own life – to embrace them and cherish them. Yours will be different from mine – different art forms, different genres, different styles and sensibilities. They are your personal pole stars – the works that can guide you through the uncharted reaches of the creative imagination and orient you on your artistic journey. And they are doubly precious if they are from an art form other than your own because they guide you without tempting you to become a copyist; they carry you to the spaces between art forms where metaphor and imagination take wing.

So open yourself to unfamiliar works in unfamiliar genres. If you are a dancer, read poetry. If you are a photographer, look at sculpture.

Find works that come at you from an oblique and unexpected angle but touch you in a way that you cannot deny. You are not looking for understanding, you are looking for connection.

When you find a work of art that resonates with

you spiritually, as Mozart's *Requiem* does with me, embrace it, learn it, make it into a friend. You have found a work that comes from the same creative source that gave birth to your own artistic vision. And when you are feeling lost or uncertain, or unsure of why you have chosen to walk the path of the artist, this work will help you remember because it sees you and knows you and meets you at the place where your spirits touch.

And where spirits touch, there is never any forgetting.

20

On the Shoulders
of Giants

The magical bond of artists
across time and space

*'Through art, mysterious bonds of understanding
and of knowledge are established among men.
They are the bonds of a great Brotherhood.
Those who are of the Brotherhood know each
other, and time and space cannot separate them.'*
Robert Henri

ONE OF THE great joys of the creative life is getting to live in dialogue with works of genius that have been created by artists who have preceded us. We observe their work across the barriers of time and space, and they become our brothers and sisters who have walked a path that shows us, however dimly, our own way forward.

I remember vividly the exhilaration I felt in my teenage years when I first encountered Antoine de Saint-Exupéry's *Night Flight*. For the first time, I realised that writing was more than topic sentences and supporting statements. I would hide under my covers at night and try, by lamplight, in my own stumbling way, to create sentences that sang like his.

And then there was the moment when I came across a stream-of-consciousness passage in John Steinbeck's *The Grapes of Wrath* that was like no prose I had read before. For weeks, in the hidden pages of my school notebooks, I struggled to describe the world around me in the same fragmentary, cinematic manner.

The experience came again as I read the works of Carl Sandburg and, later, studied the sculptures of Donatello. These artists spoke to me across time and space and became my secret friends and mentors. In my heart of hearts I dreamed of creating like they could create, and I did what I could to learn the secrets that lived inside their works.

We who work in the arts stand unashamedly upon the shoulders of those who came before. In the secrecy of our creative lives we try to do what those who inspire us have done. We trace their lines, we copy their movements; we mimic their prose, we practise their phrasings. Whether with a brush or a chisel, our body or a pen or our voices, we try to enter into their creative decisions by recreating those decisions in our own work.

It is not mere copying; it is mentoring. It is letting our hands and hearts and minds be guided by theirs. To know how Nureyev achieved the muscularity of his expression, or how Donatello carved a wrist, or how Willie Nelson phrased a song, we must attempt it ourselves. We must inhabit the experience and try to make it our own in order to see the choices that were made. We must let their artistic choices illuminate ours. We are, in effect, letting them become our teachers.

In that moment of quiet mentorship, we are closer to those artists who inspire us than we are to the people around us. We are carrying on an intimate and private dialogue with a great teacher. 'Why did you make this choice? What caused you to choose this description? Why did you deliver this line in this way?'

This intense personal dialogue allows us to live in a dimension few others ever experience. A filmmaker looking at the work of Eisenstein or watching the play of light and shadow in the work of Orson Welles is sitting in the very presence of these artists, not as artefacts or historical figures but as mentors and fellow creators. The dross of everyday life falls away, the struggles and compromises of ordinary living disappear, and in their place arises the incandescent presence of artistic genius.

This is a rare and beautiful experience that all artists know but few on the outside ever see. It makes us part of a brotherhood and sisterhood that reaches across time and space, and gives us the cherished gift of human companionship.

It is one of the true joys of a life in the arts. Once you have given yourself to an art, in the deepest part of your heart you will never be alone.

21

The Fist in
the Velvet Glove

The dream of a better world

'Painting is not done to decorate apartments.
It is an instrument of war'
Pablo Picasso

'Songs have overthrown kings and empires'
Anatole France

WE ARTISTS ARE dreamers. We see the world not as it is, but as it could be. Our imaginations breathe new life into the ordinary and give shape to the shapeless. We imagine a different world, perhaps a better world, and we want to share this world with others.

Sometimes our dreams are bright and visionary. We want to celebrate the beauty of life and change the way people experience the world. But sometimes they have a darker tinge. We see the injustice and inequities all around us and want to speak out against them. We don't simply want to change the way people experience the world, we want to change the world itself.

If you are someone who dreams of having your

art change the world, you are part of a long and honourable tradition. From Aristophanes, Goya, and Upton Sinclair, to Gil Scott-Heron and contemporary hip-hop musicians, artists across the centuries have raised their voices to speak out against the injustices of human society in the hope of creating a better world.

Sometimes those voices have spoken directly and pointedly, like Rachel Carson in her environmental treatise *Silent Spring* and Ralph Ellison in his novel *Invisible Man*. Other times, they have spoken more subtly and symbolically, like the Renaissance artists who hid their political meanings behind the symbolism of animals, or Chinese painters during the Cultural Revolution who used the image of rain to embody political oppression.

Sometimes they have served their causes merely by casting an artistic light on wrongs and social conditions, like the stunning photographs by Dorothea Lange that revealed the desperate plight of dust bowl migrants and Japanese internment camps. Other times they have sought to give voice to the voiceless, like

Studs Terkel in his amazing oral history *Working*.

But no matter how they chose to serve their causes, they knew that art had a unique power to create social change because it can focus attention on an issue or a cause in a way that almost nothing else can.

Think of Bob Dylan's 'Times They Are A-Changin" or Nick Ut's photograph of the terrified nine-year-old Vietnamese girl running naked from the US napalm attack. These works took diffuse attitudes and social concerns and gave them a singular expression that could take root in people's imaginations. They galvanised consciousness and became the rallying points for movements of political and social change.

These are political and social art at its most potent. They coalesced consciousness and articulated a sentiment in a way that touched a taproot of human feeling. They embedded themselves in our memory and became anthems and icons and true engines of social change.

If you dream of changing the world with your art, there is one caution I would like to offer. It applies to the creation of all art, but it is especially salient in the creation of art with a political or social purpose: beware of confusing shock with art.

Shock is an easy seduction because works that shock draw attention, and getting attention for your message is what you want if you hope to change hearts and minds. But we dare not mistake the response to the work for the content of the work. Good art that is truly shocking and unexpected is a real revelation and can lead to meaningful social change; work that has no content other than its shock value is a Potemkin village – a false front with nothing behind it.

Years ago I was working in an art school where a committed young student cut down all the trees in a plaza one night in order to, as she said, 'challenge the viewers to re-examine their own relationship to nature'. She claimed it was a work of political art because it created awareness of a social issue. But in reality she was creating nothing but outrage. She could have been slashing tyres or burning down houses or lighting kittens on fire. There was no focused message, no artistic centre, no aesthetic framing. Despite her efforts to wrap language around the event to give it meaning, she changed no one's mind, she opened no one's heart; her work reflected no aesthetic values. Her effort at political art was, at best, an act of social defiance; at worst, a wanton act of vandalism.

How far this was from a work like Claude Lanzmann's astonishing nine-and-a-half-hour documentary *Shoah*, where he makes us stare, without external commentary, at the profoundly ordinary reality of those who built the gas chambers and manned the railroad stations and performed the everyday tasks surrounding the operation of the Third Reich. By relentlessly holding our attention through pacing, camera work, and brilliant editing, he made us experience the lives of ordinary people caught up in a moment of history in a way that we had never encountered before. His work didn't just shock, it revealed. It actually changed our understanding by offering us a new way to see the world.

This is political and socially conscious art of the highest order. It shocks us and surprises us, but it infuses the light of artistry into the darkness of its subject. It is politics in a velvet glove.

If you truly would have your work serve the purpose of political activism or social change, you need to understand the importance of wrapping your concerns in the velvet glove of artistry. It is what gives art its unique power as a tool of social change.

Think of the righteous anger of hip-hop musicians who want to express their outrage at racial injustice and political oppression. They may verbally assault us with their political message, but they do it with rhythm and meter and internal rhyme. Their work becomes more than simple assault because it infuses the light of artistry into what can otherwise be dark and violent social commentary.

Picasso's *Guernica* is a beautifully constructed work of visual art, independent of its political message, but who among us can encounter this painting without having this image of the horrors of war forever emblazoned in our memory?

Other artists are more subtle, both in their intent and execution, but no less committed to social and political concerns. August Wilson and Arthur Miller offer their message through symbolism, allegory and the grace of a story well told. But you leave the theatre with a new understanding. You are, quite literally, moved to a new awareness by what you have encountered. You are changed, you are not just outraged.

There is no doubt that shock has its place in the creation of art, both political and otherwise. It is a powerful way to draw attention to a subject or a cause. But you do not want to just draw people's attention, you want to hold their attention. A loud noise can bring people running, but when they get there, there must be something to see.

Remember that behind your art lives the dream of a better world. You want to change hearts, not just open minds. The magic of art is that it injects music into the prose of politics and social activism. It draws people to it with the universality of its language. It does not push them away.

All of us have different degrees of social and political concern, and a different sense of urgency about the need to communicate that concern. Some of us see a world that needs to change now, and we will put ourselves and our art on the line to help achieve that change. Others of us just want our work to inject an element of kindness and awareness into the lives of those around us.

But wherever you stand – whether you dream of having your work become an icon of social change, or only of raising up people whose voices need to be heard, or shedding light on issues that need to be recognised – you must never forget that your real gift is your artistry: you are a bringer of light, not just a bringer of heat.

Wrap your cause in the velvet glove of art and people will come to it, even if they do not share your social concerns or your political commitment. They will feel the love of what you do as strongly as your outrage at what you see. For it is love that is at the heart of any art truly made; and love – not politics, not anger, not social commitment, not outrage – that, in the last analysis, will change the world.

22

The Voice that Cannot Be Stilled

Why art matters in a world of human need

'To send light into the depths of the human heart
— that is the artist's calling.'
Robert Schumann

'It is the artists of this world, the feelers
and thinkers, who will ultimately save us,
who can articulate, educate, defy, insist,
sing, and shout the big dreams.'
Leonard Bernstein

I ONCE HEARD a musician from a war-torn country reflect on the value of art during difficult times.

'Can art feed the hungry?' he asked. 'Can it stop a bullet? Would the world be better served if I gave up my music and devoted my life to meeting the human need I see around me?'

All caring artists must confront this issue at some point in their lives. With so much human need in the world – so much hunger, so much suffering – is making art a frivolous and unnecessary pursuit? Would our time not be better spent setting our hands to feeding the hungry? Helping the helpless? Consoling the inconsolable?

Perhaps if your work is overtly political or directed

toward social change you do not wrestle with this. But for those for whom the practice of art is essentially a personal quest or a search for meaning or beauty, the question is real: Is art important? Does art matter?

The answer, I believe, lies in the deepest part of the human psyche.

Imagine, if you can, the earliest days of our species, when we were emerging from our dark animal origins into the light of human awareness. Think of those first rudimentary movements toward human consciousness, when we lifted our eyes from the elemental tasks of meeting our survival needs and began to contemplate the meaning in the stars and our place in a larger universe.

How did we give expression to these earliest dawnings of the imagination?

We sang, we danced, we told stories, we drew images on cave walls – primal stirrings, elemental urges to somehow reach beyond ourselves, perhaps to call down power, perhaps to honour some inchoate sense of an ultimate 'other', perhaps to articulate some yearning inside ourselves that we could not understand.

We cannot today imagine the consciousness of those first humans or the elemental world that they inhabited. With no history, no writing, rudimentary language, and almost no awareness of their physical context beyond the small area where they carried on their lives, they were almost a species apart. Yet the creations they made are as recognisable to us as works from our own hand.

The cave paintings at Lascaux and Altamira have a grace and lyricism the equal of anything we create today. *Venus of Willendorf* speaks eloquently of symmetry and fecundity. We can imagine that the dances around fires in the forests of ancient Europe were not so different from the ecstatic twirling of the Sufis or the lyrical movements of a ballerina today.

These were not aesthetic ideas, not decorations, not entertainments. They were stirrings of the nascent human imagination, simulacra designed to summon power from some source outside the realm of human understanding. They were worship, they were celebration, they were supplication.

Now, imagine bringing those same creators forward

to today. They would not recognise our language, would not understand our thought; they would be like aliens in our modern life. But they would see in our art something that they understood, something that would call forth their assent, even as we can give assent to the creations from their hands. We could give them a brush and place them before a canvas, or sit beside them at a drum, and we would recognise each other through the works that we made.

This is how deep the urge toward artistic expression runs in the human species, and how universal and timeless it is in that expression. There is simply something fundamental in the human spirit that yearns to reach beyond itself, and it finds its voice in the creation of art.

If this urge toward expression is fundamental in the species, it is no less fundamental in each of us as individuals. Think of childhood, the time of greatest innocence, when we act without reflection or self-assessment. What is it we see when we watch a child, unobserved?

A young girl dancing. A child running to its mother

with crayons and paper, saying, 'Let's draw!' A young boy stalking across the room with a clenched face and his hands held like claws, declaring, 'I'm a monster.' A toddler sitting in the noonday sun, singing.

Artists all. Creators, unselfconscious and fearless, never saying, 'I know this isn't very good,' but full of excitement and in love with expression for its own sake. Joy, simple joy. And knowing no boundaries of time or space or gender or race.

This is the world from which we all come. We are its inheritors and its caretakers. It is our childhood joy and innocence carried forth into the harsh world of adulthood, where it stands against the divisions and animosities that surround us. It is our taproot to what is most fundamental in our human species.

Even religion, the other great universal urge of the human spirit, finds itself fraught with divisions when it seeks to give voice to what is common. But art alone reaches across all boundaries, transcends all language, transcends all time, and in some fundamental way makes us all one because it comes from our common source.

No, art cannot stop a bullet or feed the hungry. But it can tell us why we must do these things because it lies at the heart of who we are as humans and reminds us what is common among us.

Because of art we hold hands across all barriers.

And, in that, art may be more than important as a human activity. It may be essential.

23

The Eternal Youth
of the Endless Imagination

The power of art to keep the heart young

'None are so old as those who have
outlived enthusiasm.'
attrib. Henry David Thoreau

'Anyone who keeps the ability to see beauty
never grows old.'
Franz Kafka

MICHELANGELO, ARGUABLY THE greatest artistic genius of all time, is rumoured to have said upon his deathbed at the age of eighty-eight, 'I regret that I have done so little for my eternal soul and that I am but beginning to learn the alphabet of my craft.'

During my days as a sculptor I used to marvel at this statement. How could a man of such unparalleled genius find his life's accomplishments so wanting? And was not the very fact of his work the labour necessary to save his eternal soul?

I could dismiss the lament about his spiritual deficiencies as the anguished cries of a man caught in the dark throes of Savonarola's Renaissance Italian

Catholicism. But what of the lament about only beginning to learn the alphabet of his craft?

As a young sculptor I had stood before the Pietà in St Peter's, created when Michelangelo was only twenty-four, and the seventeen-foot-tall *David*, crafted with mallet and chisels from a flawed block of marble when he was but twenty-six – not to mention the Sistine Chapel and *The Last Judgment* and the spiritually luminous Pietàs of his later years – and had seen an expression of genius not matched by anyone in any art form in my experience. Not Beethoven, not Leonardo, not Bach, not Milton or Shakespeare or Rumi or Hokusai. Michelangelo simply had done things that were not imaginable by an ordinary mortal. How could he, so far beyond anything I could dream even at my most elevated and visionary, look at his life's work and see limitation and deficiency?

It was not until I was older and began to see those around me weary of the life's work they had chosen that I began to understand that there was a beautiful truth for all artists beneath Michelangelo's dark pronouncements. Behind his anguish was an unquenchable yearning for future accomplishment. He was saying, in his own tortured way, 'Wait. Wait. I still have more to learn. I still have more to offer. I am not yet done.'

In most professions there is a recognisable internal rhythm that shapes your working life. You decide what you want to do, you confront the challenges of learning how to do it, you refine the skills needed to do it well, then your familiarity and mastery allow you to proceed with calm professionalism until time and repetition take the edge off your excitement and you enter a time of quiescence, characterised by either calm acceptance and satisfaction or weary resolution. It is an entirely natural rhythm that pervades almost all of life, from our careers to our relationships to the biological progression of the natural world around us.

But for the artist this rhythm does not exist. Your career may follow this rhythm and arc, but not your active life as a creator. Each creation poses new questions and each work drives you forward with new curiosity. Your imagination and your urge toward new creation never give you easy rest.

As an artist, you are a creature of your senses. You have trained your eye to see beauty, your ear to hear music; you see patterns where others see nothing; you see the extraordinary in the ordinary. Life itself is your raw material, and life does not cease as your years increase and your senses dim. You cannot shut off the creative urge or stop the flow of ideas. Even if you cease composing music or painting canvases you will never cease hearing the music around you or seeing images in the world that passes before you. You have an artist's eye and an artist's heart. You are afflicted with the joyful curse of an endlessly curious imagination.

What does change, though, is the way you understand the art that lives undiminished in your heart. The risks you took early in your career were aimed at success. The risks you take as you get older are aimed at expression. Your work begins to look inward. It becomes less about who you want to be and more about who you are.

You find that you are more amazed by the ordinary moments in life. Everything seems more like a miracle. You really don't care if you are God's hand-maiden or God's fool. You just want to bear witness. And you want to do it in the most authentic voice possible.

This inner compulsion toward authenticity is liberating, even as it bears a heavier weight of responsibility. Concerns about success fade into concerns about legacy and moral accountability. 'Did what I do matter? Have I given all that I can give? Have the works I've created been worthy of the time I have been given?'

These concerns haunt you, in your own way and your own language, just as they haunted Michelangelo. For you, alone, know the journey you have made – what you have sacrificed, what you have accomplished, what you have left undone or unsaid. Time is no longer your ally, but you still see a world that calls out for expression.

You walk through a field and see the colours and the textures of the trees, and they form a pattern in your mind. You hear the sound of the wind and the distant voices of children and they become music. You see people talking and laughing together in a park, and your imagination turns those unheard conversations into stories. Even if your eyes have dimmed and you are no longer able to see outlines, where others feel this as diminished capacity and visual deficiency, you see a Turner-esque landscape of splashes of light and colour. Your curiosity cannot be quelled; your imagination cannot be stilled. Always there is more, always there is something new, always there is something that cries out to be given voice.

And very often, what is crying out for expression is something that only the gift of age could have revealed.

Michelangelo's Pietà Rondanini, the last piece he ever created and the sculpture on which he was working when he died, is a technical ruin. The remnant of another image, begun and abandoned, lives in the same block, and the faces are crudely rendered and indistinct. Yet the work cries out with compassion as the figure of the mother and son meld into each other and fight not to be pulled into the earth by the sheer force of gravity. Michelangelo could not have created this work until he was feeling the pull of death himself, and though his eyesight was poor and his hand was weak, he gave us a work of spiritual power and insight that only someone facing the imminent presence of death could have created.

Richard Strauss's 'Four Last Songs' do the same, offering us a quietism and reflection that comes from the very end of life but is alive with the freshness of new discovery – a discovery that is built upon a wisdom gained only as all else that mattered in life is being lost.

For others, the insights of age are less moral than aesthetic. They have new eyes, new ears, new minds, made new by the changes that come from altered skills and perception. What might seem like diminution to most of us is but a new way of seeing the world to such people. It is not about loss, it is about change, and change brings with it the excitement of new possibility. Monet's cataracts gave him the water lilies. Georgia O'Keeffe's failing eyesight made her turn to sculpting because it brought the world from the distance of her eyes to the closeness of her touch.

Beethoven's deafness may well have been the source of the difficult and deeply personal nature of the last string quartets.

This is the great irony and one of the great joys of the artistic life: decreased capacity becomes new discovery, and new discovery offers new opportunity.

'None are so old as those who have outlived enthusiasm,' Thoreau said.

For those of us in the arts, enthusiasm is never outlived. The sun is always rising before us, and our wonder at the world, which is the true source for all meaningful art, only grows stronger as life slows from passage to moments because we are able to embrace those moments more fully and want to hallow them with our art.

For those of you in your youth, this consolation may seem distant and of little note. But as the years progress and you see those around you beginning to look upon their lives as things that have passed, you realise that you possess a pearl of great price – an endless enthusiasm for creations not yet made and insights not yet expressed.

The world, which renews itself each day, renews your interest with each sunrise, and you discover that you have been given one of the greatest gifts that life has to offer: though you continue to age, you never grow old.

Coda

Expressing the Inexpressible

'If I can stop one heart from breaking,
I shall not live in vain.'
Emily Dickinson

I HAVE SPOKEN much, perhaps too much, about the difficulties and challenges of a life in the arts. But I have done so for a reason. I know too well the heaviness of the burden and the elusive nature of the dream, and I want to let you know that I understand, and that you are not alone.

But I hope I have spoken, too, of the joys and the magic of this life and have given you a vision of the world that awaits you when you give yourself to it. It is a life unlike any other, and those of you who choose it are privileged to live inside this rare and magical realm.

Still, the life of the artist is not easy.

The world will not understand you. It will praise

you too much and respect you too little. It will see the grace that you have struggled so hard to achieve in your work and assume that it came easily or is the result of God-given talent.

It will assume that you are indifferent to the worldly concerns of finances and economic survival and think that the satisfaction of living a creative life is compensation enough.

It will look upon you with envy because you get to live the life of the creator and regard you with jealousy because you appear to avoid the dross of an ordinary life.

It will distort you in ways you cannot imagine.

Though these difficulties will weigh on you, they are a small price to pay for the gifts you have been given.

You have learned to see the world with mindfulness because in the life of an artist no moment is insignificant.

You have been kept from cynicism because you know that work based on cynicism is heartless and callow.

You have known the gift of conversing with people

from different times and different lands because art is a language of the heart, and the heart is universal.

Most of all, you have been given the gift of endless youth because your life is based upon curiosity, and the curious never get old.

These are no small gifts and you should embrace them with pride. For even if your work seems small and your accomplishments insignificant, you are a part of the tribe of endless dreamers, the bearers of the cultural imagination, the shapers of the vision of what life could be.

Who else can go to the farthest reaches of the imagination to bring back new meaning and put it into physical form? Who else can bring a mindfulness to life that is celebratory, not clinical?

Who else can show us that nothing is insignificant, no one is without a story, and can call us to look at the everyday with a compassionate heart?

Who else can make us pause in our headlong rush through time to look closely at a moment, hallowing it with our attention?

Who else can re-envision the ordinary?

We artists are among the few who can bring these gifts. And we all own this legacy, no matter how great or small the works that come from our hand.

Embrace this role. You have trained your eye to see beauty, your ear to hear music. You have learned to shape meaning from chaos, to see pattern and order where others see nothing. You spin gold from straw and create life where none existed before.

I often think of the words of Martha Graham, the American dancer and choreographer. 'There is only one of you in all of time,' she said, and 'There is a vitality, a life force, an energy, a quickening that is translated through you into action.

'If you block it . . . the world will not have it. It is not your business to determine how good it is nor how valuable nor how it compares with other expressions . . . You do not even have to believe in yourself or your work. You have to keep yourself open and aware to the urges that motivate you.

'No artist is pleased . . . there is only a queer divine dissatisfaction, a blessed unrest that keeps us marching and makes us more alive than the others.'

Trust that blessed unrest. Keep yourself marching. Keep that force alive in you and continue to remind us by your work of life's creative mystery and the richness of human possibility.

This is the joyful burden, the important burden, far beyond the small difficulties and challenges that weigh on our days. You are an artist, and it is a way of the heart.

Let me leave you now with a story from my own life. It is as close as I can come to telling you why this artistic life matters and why you should embrace it.

As my mother lay dying, I was overcome with a grief and pain that was beyond anything within my imagining. I could cry, I could rail against the universe, I could sob and grieve and plead and pray, but I could do nothing to change the reality of her passing.

I was drowning. And when we are drowning, we grasp at what we can.

I am a writer. So I did what a writer does. I wrote.

I had no other voice for what was inside me. Had I been a runner, I could have run; a singer, I could have sung; a cellist, I could have made my instrument cry. But I was a writer and that was all I had to give.

So I left my mother's bedside and walked outside to stare at the sky and get away, just for a moment, from the weight of that room that was so filled with her dying.

And I wrote.

Here is what I said:

This is what is hardest: to be outside.

To see the sun, the clouds, and know that you are inside a room, inside yourself, too occupied with your dying and too weak to be brought out into the simple beauty of the daylight.

I do not want to have this pleasure; I want you to have this pleasure. I want you to feel the breeze, to see the stars, to sense the warm touch of the wind, not the cold edge of sterile sheets.

How is it we must become so small in our dying, concerned with such things as drawing a breath, or moving a hand? Why is it we cannot expand into the infinite before our final passage, to have a glimpse of what is before us, rather than only the oppressive weight of what it is we are leaving?

Perhaps you are having that glimpse; I do not know. I know only that the immediacy of pain is claiming the surface of your mind.

These are not the memories I want of you, and these are not the thoughts I want to occupy your passage. I want this to be a golden transit, a loosing of the bonds, a release, like the discarding of a gossamer veil.

I want to see you set free, like the souls of the dead in medieval paintings, flying upward to a God unquestioned, to be taken in eternal embrace and given easy rest. I want there to be relatives, ancestors, the open arms of your parents, old pets, old friends. I want this to be a reunion of all who have passed, not a descent into darkness.

Yes, it is light that I want. Light, not darkness. Yet death feels like the coming of night.

Is this me, or is this how it is? It does not matter so long as your passage is into peace. What remains for us behind is but the bones and shards, slowly *reconfigured into memories and meaning. We will do fine, here, with the roof ripped off our days, and we will find the earth again. But what will you find as you fly free? Who will you become? And what will we know of each other across this dark veil?*

I remember Father's passing not so many years ago, and the transformation of his infirm presence into the memory of his strength and goodness. I remember feeling, in my grief, that instant when he entered into me, not like a spirit but like a presence, infusing my whole being with something that I had not known before. In that instant, I became him.

I watch now, as you labour in your final breaths, and wonder how it will be when you are set free, when I become you.

I wrote until the fire burned out.

Then I went back and sat by my mother, dying.

* * *

Out of the pain and tears this was what I could create. It did not even begin to articulate the cry in my heart. But it is what I could do.

And it was the artist speaking. Not the author, not the writer of books. The artist.

It was a man taking such tools as were at his command and using them to shape the unspeakable into something that had external form. It was me trying to do with my art what art does best: express the inexpressible.

In its own way, my desolate cry into the void was no different than a teenager pouring out poems of love or grief in the private darkness of a lonely night, or a child sobbing for the loss of a pet.

That I had more tools at my command was of no significance. It was not about what I created; it was about the unburdening, the using of art to give shape to the shapeless.

Our lives are governed by necessity and practicality, our days laden with burdens and obligations. It is where the foot walks, not where the heart sings.

And then, suddenly there is a moment.

A mother dies.

We fall in love.

A child is born.

A sunset reduces us to tears.

Feelings come to us – honest feelings, human feelings, feelings that do not fit inside our square-cornered life. We want to cry out – from joy, from terror, from grief, from some emotion that wells up and overwhelms us – and we are, for a moment, in a place that has no shape and no edges; a place that expands toward the infinite and breaks all bonds of human understanding.

This is when we turn to art, because art can give shape to that moment.

Art gave me a way to grieve my mother. Art can allow you to sing the birth of your child, or dance the joy of a fresh and overwhelming love.

If we are fortunate enough to have the tools to create art that gives form to that moment, it is a treasure beyond compare. If we are able to shape that moment in a way that communicates to others, we are twice blessed.

My life has been changed – even transformed – by the *Sanctus* in Bach's Mass in B minor and the last movement of Mahler's second symphony – works that reduce me to tears and tell me my heart is not alone. Dylan Thomas's 'Fern Hill'. Robert Frost's 'Out, Out—'. These works pull a great affirmation from me, a profound and joyful 'Yes!' They make me more fully and deeply human.

These works may mean nothing to you. But somewhere there is a work created by a human hand that touches you and pulls something from you and is a touchstone for your own spiritual understanding. It is an affirmation of your experience of life.

To affirm, to articulate, to console, to inspire – these are the great gifts of the arts. They let the light shine through the confusion of life and remind us that there is something more – a mystery that can only be touched but never understood.

But above all, they provide the greatest gift that any experience can offer.

They tell us that we are part of the human family.

Acknowledgements

I ALWAYS DISLIKE writing acknowledgements, not because I think they aren't important, but because, like invitations to the wedding, they often seem more significant for whom they leave out than whom they include.

And, as someone whose understanding of life has been shaped by random encounters and small epiphanies, how do I properly acknowledge the teacher who completely altered the awareness of a twelve-year-old boy by pointing out that he started every sentence with the word 'I', or the professor who counselled the twitching, tortured graduate student to have the courage to leave the confines of academia because he himself had always wanted to be a concert pianist and had spent his life wondering how good he might have been? They, and so many others, lie in the background, unnoticed and unacknowledged, shaping the man who shaped the book, and placing my rudder in the water in ways that even now I only dimly understand.

Still, credit must be given where it is due, and it is best done by cutting a straight line through the actual process of creating the book.

To my friend, Robert Plant, who carried my work across the ocean and handed it to the very wise Andrew O'Hagan, who brought it to the attention of Canongate Books. To Jamie Byng, Canongate's incredibly creative and iconoclastic publisher, who was fascinated enough by the work of someone in the colonies to consider bringing that voice back to the motherland. To Joe Durepos, my extremely smart friend and agent, who placed the manuscript of *Dancing with the Gods* in Canongate's hands. To

Hannah Knowles, my patient, thoughtful editor, and her conscientious colleagues Leila Cruickshank and Aa'Ishah Hawton who shepherded the book from rough draft to final form.

And thanks, too, to those in my more personal circle who played their part, either by inspiration or support, in bringing *Dancing with the Gods* to life. To my wonderful wife, Louise Mengelkoch, who knows enough to stay out of the way as I bang around in my mental attic, trying to find materials worth bringing out into the light. To Michael Hoppe, musician and friend, whose insights always keep me from veering too far off course. To my son, Nik, and his young artist friends whose struggles in these difficult times inspired this book. And to Lucie, my geriatric yellow Lab, whose need for four daily walks structures my life as surely as the canonical hours, and perhaps with as much effect.

My gratitude to each of you. Your hand (and paw) prints are everywhere in these pages.

Permissions credits